REMEMBERING
THOMAS CHATTERTON

A COLLECTION OF
COMMEMORATIONS AND WRITINGS

By

VARIOUS

Read &' Co.

Copyright © 2020 Read & Co. Books

This edition is published by Read & Co. Books,
an imprint of Read & Co.

This book is copyright and may not be reproduced or copied in any
way without the express permission of the publisher in writing.

British Library Cataloguing-in-Publication Data
A catalogue record for this book is available
from the British Library.

Read & Co. is part of Read Books Ltd.
For more information visit
www.readandcobooks.co.uk

"Paint me an angel, with wings, and a trumpet,
To trumpet my name over the world."

—Thomas Chatterton

CONTENTS

SONNET TO CHATTERTON

By John Keats

O Chatterton! how very sad thy fate!
Dear child of sorrow — son of misery!
How soon the film of death obscur'd that eye,
Whence Genius mildly falsh'd, and high debate.
How soon that voice, majestic and elate,
Melted in dying numbers! Oh! how nigh
Was night to thy fair morning. Thou didst die
A half-blown flow'ret which cold blasts amate.
But this is past: thou art among the stars
Of highest heaven: to the rolling spheres
Thou sweetly singest: nought thy hymning mars,
Above the ingrate world and human fears.
On earth the good man base detraction bars
From thy fair name, and waters it with tears.

THOMAS CHATTERTON

1752-1770

A Biography from
1911 Encyclopædia Britannica, Volume 6

An English poet, was born at Bristol on the 20th of November 1752. His pedigree has a curious significance. The office of sexton of St Mary Redcliffe, at Bristol, one of the most beautiful parish churches in England, had been transmitted for nearly two centuries in the Chatterton family; and throughout the brief life of the poet it was held by his uncle, Richard Phillips. The poet's father, Thomas Chatterton, was a musical genius, somewhat of a poet, a numismatist, and a dabbler in occult arts. He was one of the sub-chanters of Bristol cathedral, and master of the Pyle Street free school, near Redcliffe church. But whatever hereditary tendencies may have been transmitted from the father, the sole training of the boy necessarily devolved on his mother, who was in the fourth month of her widowhood at the time of his birth. She established a girls' school, took in sewing and ornamental needlework, and so brought up her two children, a girl and a boy, till the latter attained his eighth year, when he was admitted to Colston's Charity.

But the Bristol blue-coat school, in which the curriculum was limited to reading, writing, arithmetic and the Church Catechism, had little share in the education of its marvellous pupil. The hereditary race of sextons had come to regard the church of St Mary Redcliffe as their own peculiar domain;

and, under the guidance of his uncle, the child found there his favourite haunt. The knights, ecclesiastics and civic dignitaries, recumbent on its altar tombs, became his familiar associates; and by and by, when he was able to spell his way through the inscriptions graven on their monuments, he found a fresh interest in certain quaint oaken chests in the muniment room over the porch on the north side of the nave, where parchment deeds, old as the Wars of the Roses, long lay unheeded and forgotten. They formed the child's playthings almost from his cradle. He learned his first letters from the illuminated capitals of an old musical folio, and learned to read out of a black-letter Bible. He did not like, his sister said, reading out of small books. Wayward, as it seems, almost from his earliest years, and manifesting no sympathy with the ordinary pastimes of children, he was regarded for a time as deficient in intellect. But he was even then ambitious of distinction. His sister relates that on being asked what device he would like painted on a bowl that was to be his, he replied, "Paint me an angel, with wings, and a trumpet, to trumpet my name over the world."

From his earliest years he was liable to fits of abstraction, sitting for hours in seeming stupor, or yielding after a time to tears, for which he would assign no reason. He had no one near him to sympathize in the strange world of fancy which his imagination had already called into being; and circumstances helped to foster his natural reserve, and to beget that love of mystery which exercised so great an influence on the development of his genius. When the strange child had attained his sixth year his mother began to recognize his capacity; at eight he was so eager for books that he would read and write all day long if undisturbed; and in his eleventh year he had become a contributor to *Felix Farley's Bristol Journal*. The occasion of his confirmation inspired some religious poems published in this paper. In 1763 a beautiful cross of curious workmanship, which had adorned the churchyard of St Mary Redcliffe for upwards of three centuries, was destroyed by a churchwarden.

The spirit of veneration was strong in the boy, and he sent to the local journal on the 7th of January 1764 a clever satire on the parish Vandal. But his delight was to lock himself in a little attic which he had appropriated as his study; and there, with books, cherished parchments, saved from the loot of the muniment room of St Mary Redcliffe, and drawing materials, the child lived in thought with his 15th-century heroes and heroines. The first of his literary mystifications, the duologue of "Elinoure and Juga," was written before he was twelve years old, and he showed his poem to the usher at Colston's hospital, Thomas Phillips, as the work of a 15th-century poet.

Chatterton remained an inmate of Colston's hospital for upwards of six years, and the slight advantages gained from this scanty education are traceable to the friendly sympathy of Phillips, himself a writer of verse, who encouraged his pupils to write. Three of Chatterton's companions are named as youths whom Phillips's taste for poetry stimulated to rivalry; but Chatterton held aloof from these contests, and made at that time no confidant of his own more daring literary adventures. His little pocket-money was spent in borrowing books from a circulating library; and he early ingratiated himself with book collectors, by whose aid he found access to Weever, Dugdale and Collins, as well as to Speght's edition of Chaucer, Spenser and other books.

His "Rowleian" jargon appears to have been chiefly the result of the study of John Kersey's *Dictionarium Anglo-Britannicum,* and Prof. W. W. Skeat seems to think his knowledge of even Chaucer was very slight.

His holidays were mostly spent at his mother's house; and much of them in the favourite retreat of his attic study there. He had already conceived the romance of Thomas Rowley, an imaginary monk of the 15th century, and lived for the most part in an ideal world of his own, in that elder time when Edward IV. was England's king, and Master William Canynge—familiar to him among the recumbent effigies in Redcliffe church—

still ruled in Bristol's civic chair. Canynge is represented as an enlightened patron of literature, and Rowley's dramatic interludes were written for performance at his house. In order to escape a marriage urged by the king, Canynge retired to the college of Westbury in Gloucestershire, where he enjoyed the society of Rowley, and eventually became dean of the institution. In "The Storie of William Canynge," one of the shorter pieces of his ingenious romance, his early history is recorded.

> "Straight was I carried back to times of yore,
> Whilst Canynge swathed yet in fleshly bed,
> And saw all actions which had been before,
>   And all the scroll of Fate unravelled;
> And when the fate-marked babe acome to sight,
> I saw him eager gasping after light.
> In all his sheepen gambols and child's play,
>   In every merrymaking, fair, or wake,
> I kenn'd a perpled light of wisdom's ray;
>   He ate down learning with the wastel-cake;
> As wise as any of the aldermen,
> He'd wit enow to make a mayor at ten."

This beautiful picture of the childhood of the ideal patron of Rowley is in reality that of the poet himself—"the fate-marked babe," with his wondrous child-genius, and all his romantic dreams realized.

The literary masquerade which thus constituted the life-dream of the boy was wrought out by him in fragments of prose and verse into a coherent romance, until the credulous scholars and antiquaries of his day were persuaded into the belief that there had lain in the parish chest of Redcliffe church for upwards of three centuries, a collection of MSS. of rare merit, the work of Thomas Rowley, an unknown priest of Bristol in the days of Henry VI. and his poet laureate, John Lydgate.

Among the Bristol patrons of Chatterton were two pewterers,

George Catcott and his partner Henry Burgum. Catcott was one of the most zealous believers in Rowley, and continued to collect his reputed writings long after the death of their real author. On Burgum, who had risen in life by his own exertions, the blue-coat boy palmed off the de Bergham pedigree, and other equally apocryphal evidences of the pewterer's descent from an ancestry old as the Norman Conquest. The de Bergham quartering, blazoned on a piece of parchment doubtless recovered from the Redcliffe muniment chest, was itself supposed to have lain for centuries in that ancient depository. The pedigree was professedly collected by Chatterton from original records, including "The Rowley MSS." The pedigree still exists in Chatterton's own handwriting, copied into a book in which he had previously transcribed portions of antique verse, under the title of "Poems by Thomas Rowley, priest of St. John's, in the city of Bristol"; and in one of these, "The Tournament," Syrr Johan de Berghamme plays a conspicuous part. The ennobled pewterer rewarded Chatterton with five shillings, and was satirized for this valuation of a noble pedigree in some of Chatterton's latest verse.

On the 1st of July 1767, Chatterton was transferred to the office of John Lambert, attorney, to whom he was bound apprentice as a clerk. There he was left much alone; and after fulfilling the routine duties devolving on him, he found leisure for his own favourite pursuits. An ancient stone bridge on the Avon, built in the reign of Henry II., and altered by many later additions into a singularly picturesque but inconvenient thoroughfare, had been displaced by a structure better adapted to modern requirements. In September 1768, when Chatterton was in the second year of his apprenticeship, the new bridge was partially opened for traffic. Shortly afterwards the editor of *Felix Farley's Journal* received from a correspondent, signing himself *Dunelmus Bristoliensis*, a "description of the mayor's first passing over the old bridge," professedly derived from an ancient MS. William Barrett, F.S.A., surgeon and antiquary, who was then accumulating materials for a history of Bristol, secured the original manuscript, which is now preserved in the British Museum, along with other Chatterton MSS., most of which were ultimately incorporated by the credulous antiquary into a learned quarto volume, entitled the *History and Antiquities of the City of Bristol*, published nearly twenty years after the poet's death. It was at this time that the definite story made its appearance—over which critics and antiquaries wrangled for nearly a century—of numerous ancient poems and other MSS. taken by the elder Chatterton from a coffer in the muniment room of Redcliffe church, and transcribed, and so rescued from oblivion, by his son. The pieces include the "Bristowe Tragedie, or the Dethe of Syr Charles Bawdin," a ballad celebrating the death of the Lancastrian knight, Charles Baldwin; "Ælla," a "Tragycal Enterlude," as Chatterton styles it, but in reality a dramatic poem of sustained power and curious originality of structure; "Goddwyn," a dramatic fragment; "Tournament," "Battle of Hastings," "The Parliament of Sprites," "Balade of Charitie," with numerous shorter pieces, forming altogether a volume of poetry, the rare merit of which is indisputable, wholly apart from the fact that it was the production of a mere boy. Unfortunately for him, his ingenious romance had either to be acknowledged as his own creation, and so in all probability be treated with contempt, or it had to be sustained by the manufacture of spurious antiques. To this accordingly Chatterton resorted, and found no difficulty in gulling the most learned of his credulous dupes with his parchments.

The literary labours of the boy, though diligently pursued at his desk, were not allowed to interfere with the duties of Mr Lambert's office. Nevertheless the Bristol attorney used to search his apprentice's drawer, and tear up any poems or other manuscripts that he could lay his hands upon; so that it was only during the absences of Mr Lambert from Bristol that he was able to expend his unemployed time in his favourite pursuits. But repeated allusions, both by Chatterton and others, seem to indicate that such intervals of freedom were of frequent occurrence. Some of his modern poems, such as the piece entitled "Resignation," are of great beauty; and these, with the satires, in which he took his revenge on all the local celebrities whose vanity or meanness had excited his ire, are alone sufficient to fill a volume. The Catcotts, Burgum, Barrett and others of his patrons, figure in these satires, in imprudent yet discriminating caricature, along with mayor, aldermen, bishop, dean and other notabilities of Bristol. Towards Lambert his feelings were of too keen a nature to find relief in such sarcasm.

In December 1768, in his seventeenth year, he wrote to Dodsley, the London publisher, offering to procure for him "copies of several ancient poems, and an interlude, perhaps the oldest dramatic piece extant, wrote by one Rowley, a priest in Bristol, who lived in the reigns of Henry VI. and Edward IV." To this letter he appended the initials of his favourite pseudonym, *Dunelmus Bristoliensis*, but directed the answer to be sent to the care of Thomas Chatterton, Redcliffe Hill, Bristol. To this, as well as to another letter enclosing an extract from the tragedy of "Ælla," no answer appears to have been returned. Chatterton, conceiving the idea of finding sympathy and aid at the hand of some modern Canynge, bethought him of Horace Walpole, who not only indulged in a medieval renaissance of his own, but was the reputed author of a spurious antique in the *Castle of Otranto*. He wrote to him offering him a document entitled "The Ryse of Peyncteyne yn Englande, wroten by T. Rowleie, 1469, for Mastre Canynge," accompanied by notes which included specimens of Rowley's poetry. To this Walpole replied with courteous acknowledgments. He characterized the verses as "wonderful for their harmony and spirit," and added, "Give me leave to ask you where Rowley's poems are to be had? I should not be sorry to print them; or at least a specimen of them, if they have never been printed." Chatterton replied, enclosing additional specimens of antique verse, and telling Walpole that he was the son of a poor widow, and clerk to an attorney, but had a taste for more refined studies; and he hinted a wish that he might help him to some more congenial occupation. Walpole's manner underwent an abrupt change. The specimens of verse had been submitted to his friends Gray and Mason, the poets, and pronounced modern. They did not thereby forfeit the wonderful harmony and spirit which Walpole had already professed to recognize in them. But he now coldly advised the boy to stick to the attorney's office; and "when he should have made a fortune," he might betake himself to more favourite studies, Chatterton had to write three times before he recovered his MSS. Walpole has been loaded with more than his just share of responsibility for the fate of the unhappy poet, of whom he admitted when too late, "I do not believe there ever existed so masterly a genius."

Chatterton now turned his attention to periodical literature and politics, and exchanged *Felix Farley's Bristol Journal* for the *Town and County Magazine* and other London periodicals. Assuming the vein of Junius—then in the full blaze of his triumph—he turned his pen against the duke of Grafton, the earl of Bute, and the princess of Wales. He had just despatched one of his political diatribes to the *Middlesex Journal*, when he sat down on Easter Eve, 17th April 1770, and penned his "Last Will and Testament," a strange satirical compound of jest and earnest, in which he intimated his intention of putting an end to his life the following evening. Among his satirical bequests, such as his "humility" to the Rev. Mr Camplin, his "religion" to Dean Barton, and his "modesty" along with his "prosody and grammar" to Mr Burgum, he leaves "to Bristol all his spirit and disinterestedness, parcels of goods unknown on its quay since the days of Canynge and Rowley." In more genuine earnestness he recalls the name of Michael Clayfield, a friend to whom he owed intelligent sympathy. The will was probably purposely prepared in order to frighten his master into letting him go. If so, it had the desired effect. Lambert cancelled his indentures; his friends and acquaintance made him up a purse; and on the 25th or 26th of the month he arrived in London.

Chatterton was already known to the readers of the *Middlesex Journal* as a rival of Junius, under the *nom de plume* of Decimus. He had also been a contributor to Hamilton's *Town and County Magazine*, and speedily found access to the *Freeholder's Magazine*, another political miscellany strong for Wilkes and liberty. His contributions were freely accepted; but the editors paid little or nothing for them. He wrote in the most hopeful terms to his mother and sister, and spent his first earnings in buying gifts for them. His pride and ambition were amply gratified by the promises and interested flattery of editors and political adventurers; Wilkes himself had noted his trenchant style, "and expressed a desire to know the author"; and Lord Mayor Beckford graciously acknowledged a political address of his, and greeted him "as politely as a citizen could." But of actual money he received but little. He was extremely abstemious, his diligence was great, and his versatility wonderful. He could assume the style of Junius or Smollett, reproduce the satiric bitterness of Churchill, parody Macpherson's Ossian, or write in the manner of Pope, or with the polished grace of Gray and Collins. He wrote political letters, eclogues, lyrics, operas and satires, both in prose and verse. In June 1770—after Chatterton had been some nine weeks in London—he removed from Shoreditch, where he had hitherto lodged with a relative, to an attic in Brook Street, Holborn. But for most of his productions the payment was delayed; and now state prosecutions of the press rendered letters in the Junius vein no longer admissible, and threw him back on the lighter resources of his pen. In Shoreditch, as in his lodging at the Bristol attorney's, he had only shared a room; but now, for the first time, he enjoyed uninterrupted solitude. His bed-fellow at Mr Walmsley's, Shoreditch, noted that much of the night was spent by him in writing; and now he could write all night. The romance of his earlier years revived, and he transcribed from an imaginary parchment of the old priest Rowley his "Excelente Balade of Charitie." This fine poem, perversely disguised in archaic language, he sent to the editor of the *Town and County Magazine,* and had it rejected.

The high hopes of the sanguine boy had begun to fade. He had not yet completed his second month in London, and already failure and starvation stared him in the face. Mr Cross, a neighbouring apothecary, repeatedly invited him to join him at dinner or supper; but he refused. His landlady also, suspecting his necessity, pressed him to share her dinner, but in vain. "She knew," as she afterwards said, "that he had not eaten anything for two or three days." But he was offended at her urgency, and assured her that he was not hungry. The note of his actual receipts, found in his pocket-book after his death, shows that Hamilton, Fell and other editors who had been so liberal in flattery, had paid him at the rate of a shilling for an article, and somewhat less than eightpence each for his songs; while much which had been accepted was held in reserve, and still unpaid for. The beginning of a new month revealed to him the indefinite postponement of the publication and payment of his work. He had wished, according to his foster-mother, to study medicine with Barrett; in his desperation he now reverted to this, and wrote to Barrett for a letter to help him to an opening as a surgeon's assistant on board an African trader. He appealed also to Mr Catcott to forward his plan, but in vain. On the 24th of August 1770, he retired for the last time to his attic in Brook Street, carrying with him the arsenic which he there drank, after tearing into fragments whatever literary remains were at hand.

He was only seventeen years and nine months old; but the best of his numerous productions, both in prose and verse, require no allowance to be made for the immature years of their author, when comparing him with the ablest of his contemporaries. He pictures Lydgate, the monk of Bury St Edmunds, challenging Rowley to a trial at versemaking, and under cover of this fiction, produces his "Songe of Ælla," a piece of rare lyrical beauty, worthy of comparison with any antique or modern production of its class. Again, in his "Tragedy of Goddwyn," of which only a fragment has been preserved, the "Ode to Liberty," with which it abruptly closes, may claim a place among the finest martial lyrics in the language. The collection of poems in which such specimens occur furnishes by far the most remarkable example of intellectual precocity in the whole history of letters. Collins, Burns, Keats, Shelley and Byron all awaken sorrow over the premature arrestment of their genius; but the youngest of them survived to his twenty-fifth year, while Chatterton was not eighteen when he perished in his miserable garret. The death of Chatterton attracted little notice at the time; for the few who then entertained any appreciative estimate of the Rowley poems regarded him as their mere transcriber. He was interred in a burying-ground attached to Shoe Lane Workhouse, in the parish of St Andrew's, Holborn, which has since been converted into a site for Farringdon Market. There is a discredited story that the body of the poet was recovered, and secretly buried by his uncle, Richard Phillips, in Redcliffe Churchyard. There a monument has since been erected to his memory, with the appropriate inscription, borrowed from his "Will," and so supplied by the poet's own pen—

"To the memory of Thomas Chatterton.
Reader! judge not. If thou art a Christian, believe that he shall be judged by a Superior Power. To that Power only is he now answerable."

MONODY ON THE DEATH OF CHATTERTON

By Samuel Taylor Coleridge

O what a wonder seems the fear of death,
Seeing how gladly we all sink to sleep,
Babes, Children, Youths, and Men,
Night following night for threescore years and ten!
But doubly strange, where life is but a breath
To sigh and pant with, up Want's rugged steep.

Away, Grim Phantom! Scorpion King, away!
Reserve thy terrors and thy stings display
For coward Wealth and Guilt in robes of State!
Lo! by the grave I stand of one, for whom
A prodigal Nature and a niggard Doom
(That all bestowing, this withholding all)
Made each chance knell from distant spire or dome
Sound like a seeking Mother's anxious call,
Return, poor Child! Home, weary Truant, home!

Thee, Chatterton! these unblest stones protect
From want, and the bleak freezings of neglect.
Too long before the vexing Storm-blast driven
Here hast thou found repose! beneath this sod!
Thou! O vain word! thou dwell'st not with the clod!
Amid the shining Host of the Forgiven
Thou at the throne of mercy and thy God

The triumph of redeeming Love dost hymn
(Believe it, O my Soul!) to harps of Seraphim.

Yet oft, perforce ('tis suffering Nature's call),
I weep that heaven-born Genius so should fall;
And oft, in Fancy's saddest hour, my soul
Averted shudders at the poison'd bowl.
Now groans my sickening heart, as still I view
Thy corse of livid hue;
Now Indignation checks the feeble sigh,
Or flashes through the tear that glistens in mine eye!

Is this the land of song-ennobled line?
Is this the land, where Genius ne'er in vain
Pour'd forth his lofty strain?
Ah me! yet Spenser, gentlest bard divine,
Beneath chill Disappointment's shade,
His weary limbs in lonely anguish lay'd.
And o'er her darling dead
Pity hopeless hung her head,
While "mid the pelting of that merciless storm,"
Sunk to the cold earth Otway's famish'd form!

Sublime of thought, and confident of fame,
From vales where Avon winds the Minstrel came.
Light-hearted youth! aye, as he hastes along,
He meditates the future song,
How dauntless ælla fray'd the Dacyan foe;
And while the numbers flowing strong
In eddies whirl, in surges throng,
Exulting in the spirits' genial throe
In tides of power his life-blood seems to flow.

And now his cheeks with deeper ardors flame,
His eyes have glorious meanings, that declare

More than the light of outward day shines there,
A holier triumph and a sterner aim!
Wings grow within him; and he soars above
Or Bard's or Minstrel's lay of war or love.
Friend to the friendless, to the sufferer health,
He hears the widow's prayer, the good man's praise;
To scenes of bliss transmutes his fancied wealth,
And young and old shall now see happy days.
On many a waste he bids trim gardens rise,
Gives the blue sky to many a prisoner's eyes;
And now in wrath he grasps the patriot steel,
And her own iron rod he makes Oppression feel.
Sweet Flower of Hope! free Nature's genial child!
That didst so fair disclose thy early bloom,
Filling the wide air with a rich perfume!
For thee in vain all heavenly aspects smil'd;
From the hard world brief respite could they win —
The frost nipp'd sharp without, the canker prey'd within!
Ah! where are fled the charms of vernal Grace,
And Joy's wild gleams that lighten'd o'er thy face?
Youth of tumultuous soul, and haggard eye!
Thy wasted form, thy hurried steps I view,
On thy wan forehead starts the lethal dew,
And oh! the anguish of that shuddering sigh!

Such were the struggles of the gloomy hour,
When Care, of wither'd brow,
Prepar'd the poison's death-cold power:
Already to thy lips was rais'd the bowl,
When near thee stood Affection meek
(Her bosom bare, and wildly pale her cheek)
Thy sullen gaze she bade thee roll
On scenes that well might melt thy soul;
Thy native cot she flash'd upon thy view,
Thy native cot, where still, at close of day,

Peace smiling sate, and listen'd to thy lay;
Thy Sister's shrieks she bade thee hear,
And mark thy Mother's thrilling tear;
See, see her breast's convulsive throe,
Her silent agony of woe!
Ah! dash the poison'd chalice from thy hand!

And thou hadst dashed it, at her soft command,
But that Despair and Indignation rose,
And told again the story of thy woes;
Told the keen insult of the unfeeling heart,
The dread dependence on the low-born mind;
Told every pang, with which thy soul must smart,
Neglect, and grinning Scorn, and Want combined!
Recoiling quick, thou badest the friend of pain
Roll the black tide of Death through every freezing vein!

O spirit blest!
Whether the Eternal's throne around,
Amidst the blaze of Seraphim,
Thou pourest forth the grateful hymn,
Or soaring thro' the blest domain
Enrapturest Angels with thy strain, —
Grant me, like thee, the lyre to sound,
Like thee with fire divine to glow; —
But ah! when rage the waves of woe,
Grant me with firmer breast to meet their hate,
And soar beyond the storm with upright eye elate!

Ye woods! that wave o'er Avon's rocky steep,
To Fancy's ear sweet is your murmuring deep!
For here she loves the cypress wreath to weave;
Watching with wistful eye, the saddening tints of eve.
Here, far from men, amid this pathless grove,
In solemn thought the Minstrel wont to rove,

Like star-beam on the slow sequester'd tide
Lone-glittering, through the high tree branching wide.

And here, in Inspiration's eager hour,
When most the big soul feels the mastering power,
These wilds, these caverns roaming o'er,
Round which the screaming sea-gulls soar,
With wild unequal steps he pass'd along,
Oft pouring on the winds a broken song:
Anon, upon some rough rock's fearful brow
Would pause abrupt — and gaze upon the waves below

Poor Chatterton! *he* sorrows for thy fate
Who would have prais'd and lov'd thee, ere too late.
Poor Chatterton! farewell! of darkest hues
This chaplet cast I on thy unshaped tomb;
But dare no longer on the sad theme muse,
Lest kindred woes persuade a kindred doom:
For oh! big gall-drops, shook from Folly's wing,
Have blacken'd the fair promise of my spring;
And the stern Fate transpierc'd with viewless dart
The last pale Hope that shiver'd at my heart!

Hence, gloomy thoughts! no more my soul shall dwell
On joys that were! no more endure to weigh
The shame and anguish of the evil day,
Wisely forgetful! O'er the ocean swell
Sublime of Hope I seek the cottag'd dell
Where Virtue calm with careless step may stray;
And, dancing to the moon-light roundelay,
The wizard Passions weave an holy spell!

O Chatterton! that thou wert yet alive!
Sure thou would'st spread the canvass to the gale,
And love with us the tinkling team to drive

O'er peaceful Freedom's undivided dale;
And we, at sober eve, would round thee throng,
Would hang, enraptur'd, on thy stately song,
And greet with smiles the young-eyed Poesy
All deftly mask'd as hoar Antiquity.

Alas, vain Phantasies! the fleeting brood
Of Woe self-solac'd in her dreamy mood!
Yet will I love to follow the sweet dream,
Where Susquehannah pours his untamed stream;
And on some hill, whose forest-frowning side
Waves o'er the murmurs of his calmer tide,
Will raise a solemn Cenotaph to thee,
Sweet Harper of time-shrouded Minstrelsy!
And there, sooth'd sadly by the dirgeful wind,
Muse on the sore ills I had left behind.

THIS IS THE 1834 EDITION
OF THE POEM AND APPEARS IN
Coleridge's last collection of poems
EDITED BY COLERIDGE'S NEPHEW

THOMAS CHATTERTON

By Henry Francis Cary

If it were allowable for one who professes to write the lives of English poets to pass the name of Chatterton in silence, I should think the literature of our country more honoured by the concealment of his fate than by the record of his genius. Yet from his brief story, the young will learn, that genius is likely to lead them into misery, if it be not accompanied by something that is better than genius; and men, whom birth and station have rendered eminent, may discover that they owe some duty to those whom nature has made more than their equals; and who—

Beneath the good tho' far—are far above the great.

Thomas Chatterton was born in the parish of St. Mary Redcliffe, at Bristol, on the twentieth of November, 1752. His father, who was of the same name, and who died about three months before the birth of his son, had been writing-master to a classical school, singing-man in Bristol cathedral, and master of the free-school in Pyle-street in that city; and is related to have been inclined to a belief in magic, and deeply versed in Cornelius Agrippa. His forefathers had borne the humble office of sexton to St. Mary Redcliffe church for a century and a half, till the death of John Chatterton, great uncle of the poet.

From what is recorded of the infancy of Chatterton, parents may be satisfied that an inaptness to learn in childhood, is far from being a prognostic of future dullness. At the age of five years, he was sent to the school of which his father had been

27

master, and was found so incorrigibly stupid, that he was rejected by the teacher, whose name was Love, as incapable of profiting by his instruction. His mother, as most mothers would have done in the like case, bitterly lamented her son's untowardness; when an old musical manuscript in French coming in his way, he fell in love, as she expressed it, with the illuminated capitals. Of this fancy she eagerly availed herself to lead him on to an acquaintance with the alphabet; and from hence proceeded to teach him to read in an old Testament or Bible in the black letter. Doctor Gregory, one of his biographers, justly observes, that it is not unreasonable to suppose his peculiar fondness for antiquities to have originated in this incident.

It is related, on the testimony of his sister, as a mark of his early thirst for distinction, that being offered a present of china-ware by a potter, and asked what device he would have painted on it, he replied, "Paint me an angel with wings, and a trumpet to trumpet my name about the world." It is so usual with those who are fondly attached to a child, to deceive themselves into a belief, that what it has said on the suggestion of others, has proceeded from its own mind, that much credit is seldom due to such marvels.

A little before he had attained his eighth year, he was admitted into Colston's charity school in Bristol, an institution in some respects similar to that excellent one of Christ's Hospital in London, the boys being boarded and clothed, as well as instructed, in the house. In two years his dislike to reading was so thoroughly overcome, that he spent the pocket-money allowed him by his mother in hiring books from a circulating library. He became reserved, thoughtful, and at times melancholy; mixed little in childish sports; and between his eleventh and twelfth years had made a catalogue of the books he had read to the number of seventy. It is to be regretted, that with a disposition thus studious, he was not instructed in any language but his own. The example of one of the assistants in the school, named Thomas Phillips, spread a poetical emulation among the elder boys, of whom Thistlethwaite, Cary, and Fowler, figured in the periodical publications of the day. Chatterton did not escape the contagion; and a pocket-book presented to him by his sister, as a new-year's gift, was returned at the end of the year filled with his writing, chiefly in verse. Phillips is probably the person whose skill in poetry is extolled by Chatterton in an elegy on the death of his acquaintance of that name, which has some stanzas of remarkable beauty.

Soon after his confirmation by the bishop, at twelve years of age, he was prompted by the serious reflections which the performance of that ceremony had awakened in him, to compose some lines on the Last Day, and a paraphrase of the ninth chapter of Job, and of some chapters in Isaiah. Had his life been protracted, there is every reason to believe, from the process which usually takes place in minds constituted like his, that after an interval of scepticism, these feelings of piety would have returned in their full force. At the same time he indulged himself in satirical effusions on his master, and such of his schoolfellows as had provoked either his resentment or his ridicule.

On the first of July, 1767, he was taken from school, and apprenticed for seven years to Mr. John Lambert, attorney, of Bristol, to be instructed in the art of a scrivener. The apprentice fee was only ten pounds; he slept in the room with the footboy, and was confined to the office from eight o'clock in the morning, with the usual interval for dinner, till the same hour at night. His conduct was such as left his master no room for blame. He never exceeded the hours limited for his absence, except on one occasion, when he had been to spend an evening in the company of his mother and some friends. Once only he incurred correction. His old schoolmaster had received an abusive anonymous letter; and Lambert having discovered from the hand-writing, which was ill disguised, and by the paper, which was the same as that used in his office, that Chatterton was the writer, thought it necessary to check so mischievous a propensity, by inflicting on him one or two blows. Though he was compelled to pass so large a portion of time in confinement, he had much leisure left him, as his master's business frequently did not occupy more than two hours in the day. His chief employment was the copying of precedents, with which he filled a folio book of 344 pages closely written.

At the beginning of October, 1768, the new bridge at Bristol was completed; and about the same time there appeared in the Bristol Journal a paper, purporting to be a description of the Fryar's first passing over the old bridge, taken from an ancient manuscript, and signed Dunhelmus Bristoliensis. By this the public curiosity was excited; and the printer not being able to satisfy the inquiries that were made concerning the quarter from whence he had received the communication, it was with some difficulty traced to Chatterton. To the menaces of those, who first roughly demanded from him an account of the means by which the paper had come into his hands, he refused to give any reply; but on being more mildly questioned, after some prevaricating, said, that he had got it, together with several other manuscripts, that had been in the possession of his father, by whom they were found in a large box, in an upper room, over the chapel, on the north side of Redcliffe church. That some old parchments had been seen by him in his mother's house is nearly certain; nor is it at all improbable that they might have been discovered in a neglected coffer in the church, according to the account he gave of them. But that either the description of the Fryar's passage over the bridge, or the most considerable of the poems attributed to Rowley were among them, can scarcely be credited. The delusion supposed to have been practised on the public by Macpherson, and that acknowledged to have been so by Walpole, in passing off the Castle of Otranto for a translation from the Italian, were then recent; and these examples might have easily engaged Chatterton to attempt a fraud, which did not seem likely to be more injurious in its consequences than either of them.

About the same time he became known to a Mr. Catrott, and to a Mr. Barrett, a chirurgeon at Bristol, who intended to publish a history of that city, and was then collecting materials for the purpose. To the former he showed the Bristowe Tragedy, the Epitaph on Robert Canynge, and some other short pieces; to the latter several fragments, some of considerable length, affirming them to be portions of the original manuscripts which had fallen into his hands. From both he received at different times some pecuniary reward for these communications, and was favoured by the loan of some books. Among those which he borrowed of Mr. Barrett, there were several on medical subjects; and from him he obtained also some instructions in chirurgery. He is represented by one of his companions to have extended his curiosity, at this time, to many other objects of inquiry; and to have employed himself not only in the lighter studies of heraldry and English antiquities, but in the theory of music, mathematics, metaphysics, and astronomy.

He now became a contributor of prose and verse to the Magazines. Among the acknowledgments to correspondents in the Town and Country Magazine for November, 1768, one of his letters appears to be noticed; but nothing of his writing in that miscellany, the first with which he is known to have corresponded, has been discovered before the February of the following year.

The attention he had drawn to himself in his native city soon induced him to aspire after higher notice. In March he addressed the following letter to the Honourable Horace Walpole;

Corn Street, Bristol,
March 25th.

SIR,—Being versed a little in antiquities, I have met with several curious manuscripts, among which the following may be of service to you in any future edition of your truly entertaining Anecdotes of Painting.

In correcting the mistakes (if any) in the notes, you will greatly oblige

Your most humble servant,

THOMAS CHATTERTON

This was accompanied by a manuscript, entitled "The Ryse of Peyneteyne in Englande, wroten by T. Rowleie, 1469, for Mastre Canynge:" to which Chatterton had annexed his own remarks. Walpole returned a polite answer, and asked for further communications. On the receipt of a second letter from Chatterton, Walpole repeated his wish to know more concerning Rowley and his poems; in reply to which, Chatterton took occasion to represent his own situation, that he was the son of an indigent widow, and clerk to an attorney, but that his inclinations led him to more elegant pursuits; and he intimated a hope that Walpole would assist in placing him where he might be able to gratify such propensities. His letter was accompanied by more of the Rowleian poems, and contained an assurance, that the person who had lent them to him to transcribe, possessed other valuable relics of ancient poetry. Some inquiries which Walpole made, confirmed the account given by Chatterton of himself; but in answer to his solicitation for patronage, Walpole declared that he had not the means of exerting it; and recommended a sedulous attention to business, as the most certain way of recompensing his mother for her care, and of securing his own independence. He mentioned that more competent judges, than he pretended to be, were not satisfied of the manuscripts being genuine; and at the same time stated their reasons for concluding them to be of another age than that to which they were assigned. Shortly after, Chatterton wrote to him two letters, which though querulous, are not disrespectful. In the first, while he thanks his correspondent for the advice he had given him, he professes his resolution "to go a little beyond it, by destroying all his useless lumber of literature, and never using his pen again but in the law;" and in the other, declaring his settled conviction that the papers of Rowley were genuine, he asks him to return the copy which had been sent him. Owing to the absence of Walpole, who was then in Paris, some time elapsed without any notice being taken of this request; and on his return Walpole found the following letter, which he terms singularly impertinent.

July 24th.

SIR,—I cannot reconcile your behaviour to me with the notions I once entertained of you. I think myself injured, Sir; and did you not know my circumstances, you would not dare to treat me thus. I have sent for a copy of the M.S. No answer from you. An explanation or excuse for your silence would oblige

THOMAS CHATTERTON.

The manuscripts and letters were all returned in a blank cover, on the fourth of August, and here the intercourse was at an end. Gray and Mason were the friends whom Walpole had consulted about the manuscripts, and they had no hesitation in pronouncing them to be forgeries. It may seem strange, that with such men, the uncommon beauty of the poetry they contained did not create some interest for the author. But Gray was now in a state of health that, perhaps, left him little power of being interested in anything; or the wonder may resolve itself into that blindness which poets, no less than patrons, too frequently discover for the excellence of their contemporaries. Chatterton himself spoke with contempt of the productions of Collins. As to Walpole, he had no doubt more pleasure in petting the lap-dog that was left to his care by the old blind lady at Paris, than he could ever have felt in nursing the wayward genius of Chatterton.

During his residence in Lambert's house, his constitutional reserve had assumed an air of gloomy sullenness: he had repeatedly betrayed to the servants an intention of committing suicide; and at length a paper, entitled the last Will and Testament of Thomas Chatterton, which was found lying on his desk, manifested a design of perpetrating this act on the ensuing day, Easter Sunday, April 15th, 1770. On so unequivocal a proof as this appeared to be of his desperate resolution, his master no longer thought it safe to retain him.

A few months before, he had written letters to several booksellers and printers in London, and from them received assurances of protection and employment if he should remove to the capital. This decided him as to his future course. When he was questioned by Thistlethwaite as to the plan of life he intended to pursue, if the prospect which was thus held out, should fail him, he answered: "The promises I have had are sufficient to dispel doubt; but should I be deceived I will turn Methodist preacher. Credulity is as potent a deity as ever, and a new sect may easily be devised. But if that too should fail me, my last and final resource is a pistol." It is almost unnecessary to observe, that when he thus speculated on his future proceedings, his mind had been strongly tainted with infidelity.—Towards the conclusion of April he set forth on his ill-omened journey. He had never yet gone farther than a Sunday's walk from his native city; and at the age of seventeen, equally inexperienced and confident, without a friend or a guide, and with principles shaken and perverted, he was about to enter on a new and perilous theatre; nor could it have been difficult to divine what the event must soon be. On the 26th of April 1770, immediately after his arrival in London, he writes to his mother, and speaks in high spirits of the encouragement he has met with from the booksellers to whom he has applied, "who," says he, "all approve of my design." On the sixth of the next month, he informs her that "he gets four guineas a month by one Magazine, and that he shall engage to write a history of England and other pieces, which will more than double that sum." "Mr. Wilkes had known him by his writings, since he first corresponded with the booksellers. He is to visit him the following week, and by his interest would ensure Mrs. Ballance the Trinity House." In short he is in raptures at the change in his condition and views; and talks as if his fortune were already made. He now inhabited the house of Walmsley, a plasterer, in Shoreditch, where his kinswoman Mrs. Ballance also lived.

The other letters to his mother and sisters betray the same intoxication. At the Chapter Coffee-house, he meets with a gentleman "who would have introduced him as a companion to the young duke of Northumberland in his intended general tour, had he not been unluckily incapacitated for that office by his ignorance of any tongue but his own. His present profession obliges him to frequent places of the best resort. He employs his money in fitting himself fashionably, and getting into good company; this last article always brings him in good interest. He has engaged to live with a gentleman, the brother of a lord (a Scotch one indeed) who is going to advance pretty deeply into the bookselling branches, and is to have lodging and boarding, genteel and elegant, gratis, besides no inconsiderable premium. He is introduced to Beckford, the Lord Mayor, to whom he had addressed an Essay, and who received him with all the politeness a citizen could assume, and warmly invited him to come again. He might have a recommendation to Sir George Colebrook, an East India Director, as qualified for an office no ways despicable; but he shall not take a step to the sea while he can continue on land. If money flowed as fast upon him as honours, he would give his sister a portion of £5000." The kind-hearted boy did indeed find means out of the little profits arising from his writings, to send her, his mother, and his grandmother, several trifling presents. In July he removed to lodgings at Mrs. Angel's, a sack-maker in Brook Street, Holborn. He assigned no reason for quitting those he had occupied in Shoreditch; but

Sir Herbert Croft supposes, not without probability, that it was in order to be nearer to the places of public entertainment, to which his employment as a writer for ephemeral publications, obliged him to resort. On the 20th of July, he acquaints his sister that he is engaged in writing an Oratorio, which when finished would purchase her a gown, and that she might depend on seeing him before the first of January, 1771. "Almost all the next Town and Country Magazine," he tells her, "is his." He boasts that "he has an universal acquaintance; that his company is courted every where; and could he humble himself to go behind a compter, he could have had twenty places, but that he must be among the great: state matters suit him better than commercial." Besides his communications to the above mentioned miscellany, he was a frequent contributor of essays and poems to several of the other literary journals. As a political writer, he had resolved to employ his pen on both sides. "Essays," he tells his sister, "on the patriotic side, fetch no more than what the copy is sold for. As the patriots themselves are searching for a place, they have no gratuities to spare. On the other hand, unpopular essays will not be accepted, and you must pay to have them printed; but then you seldom lose by it. Courtiers are so sensible of their deficiency in merit, that they generally reward all who know how to daub them with an appearance." But all his visions of emolument and greatness were now beginning to melt away. He was so tired of his literary drudgery, or found the returns it made him so inadequate to his support, that he condescended to solicit the appointment of a chirurgeon's mate to Africa, and applied to Mr. Barrett for a recommendation, which was refused him, probably on account of his incapacity. It is difficult to trace the particulars of that sudden transition from good to bad fortune which seems to have befallen him. That his poverty was extreme cannot be doubted. The younger Warton was informed by Mr. Cross, an apothecary in Brook Street, that while Chatterton lived in the neighbourhood, he often called at his shop; but though pressed by Cross to dine or sup with him, constantly declined the invitation, except one evening, when he was prevailed on to partake of a barrel of oysters, and ate most voraciously. A barber's wife who lived within a few doors of Mrs. Angel's, gave testimony, that after his death Mrs. Angel told her, that "on the 24th of August, as she knew he had not eaten anything for two or three days, she begged he would take some dinner with her; but he was offended at her expressions, which seemed to hint that he was in want, and assured her he was not hungry." The stripling whose pride would not let him go behind a compter, had now drunk the cup of bitterness to the dregs. On that day he swallowed arsenic in water, and on the following expired. His room was broken into, and found strewn over with fragments of papers which he had destroyed. He was interred in the burying-ground of Shoe Lane work-house. Such was the end of one who had given greater proofs of poetical genius than perhaps had ever been shown in one of his years. By Johnson he was pronounced "the most extraordinary young man that had ever encountered his knowledge;" and Warton, in the History of English Poetry, where he discusses the authenticity of the Rowleian poems, gives it as his opinion, that Chatterton "would have proved the first of English poets if he had reached a maturer age."

"He was proud," says his sister, "and exceedingly imperious;" but both she and his school-fellow Thistlethwaite, vindicated him from the charge of libertinism, which was brought against him by some who thought they could not sufficiently blacken his memory. On the contrary, his abstemiousness was uncommon; he seldom used animal food or strong liquors, his usual diet being a piece of bread and a tart, and some water. He fancied that the full of the moon was the most propitious time for study, and would often sit up and write the whole night by moonlight. His spirits were extremely uneven, and he was subject to long and frequent fits of absence, insomuch that he would look stedfastly in a person's face without speaking or seeming to see him for a quarter of an hour or more. There is said to have been something peculiarly pleasing in his manner and address. His person was marked by an air of manliness and dignity that bespoke the superiority of his mind. His eyes, one of which was more remarkable than the other, were of a grey colour, keen, and brilliant, especially when any thing occurred to animate him. Of all the hypotheses concerning those papers which have been the subject of so much controversy, none seems more probable than that suggested by Warton, who, in the History of English Poetry, admits that some of the poems attributed to Rowley might have been preserved in Canynge's chest; and in another publication allows that Chatterton "might have discovered parchments of humble prose containing local memoirs and authentic deeds illustrating the history of Bristol, and biographical diaries, or other notices, of the lives of Canynge, Ischam, and Gorges. But that many of the manuscripts were not genuine, is proved not only by the dissimilitude of the style to any composition of the age of Henry VI. and Edward IV. and by the marked resemblance to several passages in modern poets, but by certain circumstances which leave little or no doubt of their having been fabricated by Chatterton himself." One of his companions, at the time that he was an apprentice to Lambert, affirms, that he one day produced a piece of parchment on which he wrote several words, if not lines, in a character that appeared to his companion totally unlike English, that he then held it over a candle to give it the appearance of antiquity, which changed the colour of the ink, and made the parchment appear black and contracted. Another person declares, that he saw him rub a piece of parchment in several places in streaks with yellow ochre, and then rub it on the ground which was dirty, and afterwards crumple it in his hand. Having concluded the operation, he said it would do pretty well, but he could do it better at home. The first part of the Battle of Hastings, he confessed to Mr. Barrett, that he had written himself.

Some anachronisms as to particular allusions have been pointed out. The irregular, or Pindaric measure as it has been called, used in the song to Aella, in the verses on the Mynster, and in the chorus in Goddwyn, was not employed till a much later aera. There are also in the Aella some lines in blank verse, not introduced among us till the time of Surrey, who adopted it from the Italian.

Another criterion of a more general nature, which has not yet, at least that I am aware, been applied to those compositions, is, I think, very strongly against the antiquity of them; and that is, that the intention and purpose of the writer in the longer pieces is not sufficiently marked and decisive for the remoter ages to which they are ascribed. In the early stages of a language, before conventional phrases have been formed, and a stock of imagery, as it were, provided for the common use, we find that the plan of a work is often rude and simple indeed, but that it almost always bears evident signs of having subsisted anteriorly in the mind of the writer as a whole. If we try Aella, the longest of the poems, by this test, we shall discover strong evidence of its being modern. A certain degree of uniformity is the invariable characteristic of the earlier productions of art; but here is as much desultoriness and incoherence, as can well he possible in a work that makes any pretensions to a plan. On this internal proof alone I should not hesitate in assigning it to Chatterton rather than to Rowley, to the one who luxuriated in an abundance of poetic materials poured out before him for his use or his imitation, rather than to the other who had comparatively but a few meagre models to work upon.

Where he is much inspirited by his subject, being thrown off his guard, he forgets himself and becomes modern, as in these lines, from which I have removed nothing but the old spelling.

First Dane

Fly, fly, ye Danes! Magnus, the chief, is slain;
The Saxons come, with Aella at their head;

Let's strive to get away to yonder green;
Fly, fly! this is the kingdom of the dead.

Second Dane

O gods! have Romans at my anlace bled?
And must I now for safety fly away?
See! far besprenged all our troops are spread,
Yet I will singly dare the bloody fray.
But no; I'll fly, and murder in retreat;
Death, blood, and fire shall mark the going of my feet.

The following repetitions are, if I mistake not, quite modern:

Now Aella *look'd*, and *looking* did exclaim;

and,

He *falls*, and *falling* rolleth thousands down.

As is also this antithetical comparison of the qualities of a war-horse to the mental affections of the rider:

Bring me a steed, with eagle-wings for fight,
Swift as my wish, and as my love is, strong.

There are sometimes single lines, that bear little relation to the place in which they stand, and seem to be brought in for no other purpose than their effect on the ear. This is the contrivance of a modern and a youthful poet.

Thy words be high of din, but nought beside,

is a line that occurs in Aella, and may sometimes be applied to the author himself.

Nothing indeed is more wonderful in the Rowley poems than the masterly style of versification which they frequently display. Few more exquisite specimens of this kind can be found in our language than the Minstrel's song in Aella, beginning,

O sing unto my roundelay.

A young poet may be expected to describe warmly and energetically whatever interests his fancy or his heart; but a command of numbers would seem to be an art capable of being perfected only by long-continued and diligent endeavours. It must be recollected, however, that much might be done in the time which was at Chatterton's disposal, when that time was undivided by the study of any other language but his own. We see, in the instance of Milton's juvenile poems in Latin, not to mention others, to what excellence this species of skill may be brought, even in boyhood, where the organs are finely disposed for the perception of musical delight; and if examples of the same early perfection be rarer in our own tongue, it may be because so much labour is seldom or ever exacted, at that age, in the use of it.

Tyrwhitt, whose critical acumen had enabled him to detect a supposititious passage in a tragedy of Euripides, was at first a dupe to the imposture of Chatterton, and treated the poems as so decidedly genuine, that he cited them for the elucidation of Chaucer; but seeing good grounds for changing his opinion, as Mr. Nichols[1] informs us, he cancelled several leaves before his volume was published. Walpole was equally deceived; though his vanity afterwards would not suffer him to own that he had been so. Mr. Tyson, in a letter to Dr. Glynn,[2] well observed, that he could as soon believe that Hogarth painted the cartoons, as that Chatterton wrote Rowley's poems: yet (he adds) they are as unlike any thing ancient, as Sir Joshua's flowing contour is unlike the squares and angles of Albert Durer.

The poems that were written after his arrival in London,

41

when his mind was agitated by wild speculations, and thrown off its balance by noise and bustle, were, as might be expected, very unequal to those which he had produced in the retirement of his native place. Yet there is much poignancy in the satires. The three African eclogues have a tumid grandeur. Heccar and Gaira is the best of them.

The following verses are strong and impassioned:

> The children of the wave, whose pallid race
> Views the faint sun display a languid face,
> From the red fury of thy justice fled,
> Swifter than torrents from their rocky bed.
> Fear with a sicken'd silver tinged their hue,
> The guilty fear where vengeance is their due.

Many of the pieces, confessedly his own, furnish descriptions of natural objects, equally happy with those so much admired in the Rowleian poems.

> When golden Autumn, wreath'd in ripen'd corn,
> From purple clusters pour'd the foamy wine,
> Thy genius did his sallow brows adorn,
> And made the beauties of the season thine.
> With rustling sound the yellow foliage flies,
> And wantons with the wind in rapid whirls,
> The gurgling rivulet to the vallies hies, ——
> Whilst on its bank the spangled serpent curls.

⁕ ⁕ ⁕ ⁕ ⁕

> Pale rugged Winter bending o'er his tread;
> His grizzled hair bedropt with icy dew;
> His eyes a dusky light congeal'd and dead,
> His robe a tinge of bright ethereal blue.

His train a motley'd, sanguine, sable cloud,
He limps along the russet dreary moor,
Whilst rising whirlwinds, blasting keen and loud,
Roll the white surges to the sounding shore.

The lofty elm, the oak of lordly look,
The willow shadowing the babbling brook,
The hedges blooming with the sweets of May,
With double pleasure mark'd the gladsome way.

In "Resignation," from which these lines are taken, there is a fine personification of Hope, though the application of it is designedly ludicrous.

See Hope array'd in robes of virgin white,
Trailing an arch'd variety of light,
Comes showering blessings on a ruin'd realm,
And shows the crown'd director of the helm.

With him poetry looks best when she is

All deftly mask'd as hoar antiquity.

Scarcely any of these later poems are free from grammatical incorrectness or ambiguity of expression. Some are debased by the more serious fault of ribaldry and profaneness. His irreligion, however, seems to have been rather the fluctuating of a mind that had lost its hold on truth for a time, than the scepticism of one confirmed in error. He acknowledges his dependence on a Creator, though he casts off his belief in a Redeemer. His incredulity does not appear so much the offspring of viciousness refusing the curb of moral restraint, as of pride unwilling to be trammelled by the opinions of the multitude. We cannot conceive that, with a faculty so highly imaginative, he could long have continued an unbeliever; or, perhaps, that he could ever have been so in his heart. But he is a portentous example of the dangers to which an inexperienced youth, highly gifted by nature, is exposed, when thrown into the midst of greedy speculators, intent only on availing themselves of his resources for their own advantage, and without any care for his safety or his peace.

Some years ago the present laureat (Southey) undertook the office of editing his works, for the benefit of his sister, Mrs. Newton. It is to be lamented, that a project so deserving of encouragement does not appear to have been successful.

A Chapter from
Lives of the English Poets, 1850

FOOTNOTES

[1] Illustrations of Literature, vol. i. p. 158.

[2] Nichols's Literary An. vol. viii. p. 640.

THOMAS CHATTERTON

By Mabel E. Wotton

WILSON'S CHATTERTON

"It is to be feared that no authentic portrait of Chatterton exists; and even the accounts furnished as to his appearance, only partially aid us in realising an idea of the manly, handsome boy, with his flashing, hawklike eye, through which even the Bristol pewterer thought he could see his soul. His forehead one fancies must have been high; though hidden, perhaps, as in the supposed Gainsborough portrait, with long flowing hair. His mouth, like that of his father, was large. But the brilliancy of his eyes seems to have diverted attention from every other feature; and they have been repeatedly noted for the way in which they appeared to kindle in sympathy with his earnest utterances. Mr. Edward Gardner, who only knew him during his last three months in Bristol, specially recalled 'the philosophic gravity of his countenance, and the keen lightening of his eye.' Mr. Capel, on the contrary, resided as an apprentice in the same house where Lambert's office was, and saw Chatterton daily.

His advances had been repelled at times with the flashing glances of the poet; and the terms in which he speaks of his pride and visible contempt for others show there was little friendship between them. But he also remarks: 'Upon his being irritated or otherwise greatly affected, there was a light in his eyes which seemed very remarkable.'

He had frequently heard this referred to by others; and Mr. George Catcott speaks of it as one who had often quailed before such glances, or been spell-bound, like Coleridge's wedding guest by the 'glittering eye' of the Ancient Mariner. He said he could never look at it long enough to see what sort of an eye it was; but it seemed to be a kind of hawk's eye. You could see his soul through it."

GREGORY'S
Life of Chatterton

"The person of Chatterton, like his genius, was premature; he had a manliness and dignity beyond his years, and there was a something about him uncommonly prepossessing. His more remarkable feature was his eyes which, though gray, were uncommonly piercing; when he was warmed in argument or otherwise, they sparked with fire, and one eye, it is said, was still more remarkable than the other."

A CHAPTER FROM
Word Portraits of Famous Writers, 1887

POEM OF
THOMAS CHATTERTON

By Dante Gabriel Rossetti

With Shakspeare's manhood at a boy's wild heart,—
Through Hamlet's doubt to Shakspeare near allied,
And kin to Milton through his Satan's pride,—
At Death's sole door he stooped, and craved a dart;
And to the dear new bower of England's art,—
Even to that shrine Time else had deified,
The unuttered heart that soared against his side,—
Drove the fell point, and smote life's seals apart.
Thy nested home-loves, noble Chatterton;
The angel-trodden stair thy soul could trace
Up Redcliffe's spire; and in the world's armed space
Thy gallant sword-play:—these to many an one
Are sweet for ever; as thy grave unknown
And love-dream of thine unrecorded face.

CURSORY OBSERVATIONS
ON THE POEMS ATTRIBUTED
TO THOMAS ROWLEY

An Essay by Edmond Malone

Never surely was the course marked out by our great Satirist–
And write about it, Goddess, and about it–more strictly followed,
than in the compositions which the present *Rowleiomania* has
produced. Mercy upon us! Two octavo volumes and a huge
quarto, to prove the forgeries of an attorney's clerk at Bristol
in 1769, the productions of a priest in the fifteenth century!—
Fortunate Chatterton! What the warmest wishes of the admirers
of the greatest Genius that England ever produced have not
yet effected, a magnificent and accurate edition of his works,
with notes and engravings, the product of thy fertile brain has
now obtained.–It is almost needless to say, that I allude to two
new publications by Mr. Bryant, and the Dean of Exeter; in
the *modest* title of one of which, *the authenticity* of the poems
attributed to Thomas Rowley is said to be *ascertained*; the
other gentleman indeed does not go so far–he only *considers
and defends their antiquity.*–Many persons, no doubt, will be
deterred by the size of these works from reading them. It is not,
however, so great as they may imagine; for Mr. Bryant's book is
in fact only a moderate octavo, though by dextrous management
it has been divided into two volumes, to furnish an excuse (as
it should seem) for demanding an uncommon price. Bulky,
however, as these works are, I have just perused them, and
entreat the indulgence of those who think the discussion of a
much controverted literary point worth attention, while I lay

49

before them some observations on this inexhaustible subject.

And, first, I beg leave to lay it down as a fixed principle, that the authenticity or spuriousness of the poems attributed to Rowley cannot be decided by any person who has not a taste for English poetry, and a moderate, at least, if not a critical, knowledge of the compositions of most of our poets from the time of Chaucer to that of Pope. Such a one alone is, in my opinion, a competent judge of this matter; and were a jury of twelve such persons empaneled to try the question, I have not the smallest doubt what would be their almost instantaneous decision. Without this critical knowledge and taste, all the Saxon literature that can be employed on this subject (though these learned gentlemen should pour out waggon instead of cart-loads of it,) will only puzzle and perplex, instead of illustrating, the point in dispute. Whether they are furnished with any portion of this critical taste, I shall now examine. But that I may not bewilder either my readers or myself, I will confine my observations to these four points. 1. The versification of the poems attributed to Rowley. 2. The imitations of modern authours that are found in them. 3. The anachronisms with which they abound.4. The hand-writing of the Mss.–the parchments, &c.

I. It is very obvious, that the first and principal objection to the antiquity of these poems is the smoothness of the versification. A series of more than three thousand lines, however disfigured by old spelling, flowing for the most part as smoothly as any of Pope's–is a difficult matter to be got over. Accordingly the learned Mythologist, Mr. Bryant, has laboured hard to prove, either, that other poets of the fifteenth century have written as smoothly, or, if you will not allow him this, that Rowley was a prodigy, and wrote better than all his contemporaries; and that this is not at all incredible, it happening very frequently. And how, think you, gentle reader, he proves his first point? He produces some verses from Spenser, written about the year 1571; some from Sir John Cheke, written in 1553; and others from Sir H. Leamaster of the Armoury to queen Elizabeth. These having not the smallest relation to the present question, I shall take no notice of them. He then cites some verses of blind Harry, (who knows not blind Harry?) written in the time of King Edward IV.; and some from *the Pilgrimage of the Soul*, printed by Caxton in 1483. I will not encumber my page by transcribing them; and will only observe, that they do not at all prove the point for which they are adduced, being by no means harmonious. But were these few verses ever so smooth, they would not serve to decide the matter in controversy. The question is not, whether in Chaucer, or any other ancient English poet, we can find a *dozen* lines as smooth as

> Wincing she was, as is a jolly colt,
> Long as a mast, and upright as a bolt–

but whether we can find *three thousand* lines as smooth as these; containing the same rythm, the very collocation and combination of words used in the eighteenth century.

Let us bring this matter to a very fair test. Any quotation from particular parts of old poetry is liable to suspicion, and may be thought to be selected by the advocates on one side as remarkably harmonious, or by those on the other as uncommonly rugged and uncouth. I will therefore transcribe the first four lines of as many ancient poems as are now lying before me; and I request that they may be compared with the opening of *the Battle of Hastings*, No I, the piece which happens to stand first in the new quarto edition of Chatterton's works.

Divested of its old spelling, which is only calculated to mislead the reader, and to assist the intended imposition, it begins thus:

> "O Christ, it is a grief for me to tell
> "How many a noble earl and val'rous knight
> "In fighting for king Harold nobly fell,
> "All slain in Hastings' field, in bloody fight."

Or, as Chatterton himself acknowledged this to be a forgery, perhaps it will be more proper to quote the beginning of *the Battle of Hastings*, N2 2, which he asserted to be a genuine, ancient composition:

"O Truth! immortal daughter of the skies,
"Too little known to writers of these days,
"Teach me, fair saint, thy passing worth to prize,
"To blame a friend, and give a foeman praise."

The first four lines of *the Vision of Pierce Plowman*, by William (or Robert) Langland, who flourished about the year 1350, are as follows:

"In a summer season, when set was the sunne,
"I shope me into shroubs, as I a shepe were,
"In habit as an hermet, unholye of werkes,
"Went wide in the Werlde, wonders to here."

Chaucer, who died in 1400, opens thus:

"Whanne that April with his shoures sote
"The droughte of March hath perced to the rote,
"And bathed every veine in swiche licour,
"Of whiche vertue engendred is the flour–."

The *Confessio Amantis* of Gower, who died in 1402, begins thus:

"I maye not stretche uppe to the heven
"Myn honde, ne set al in even
"This worlde, whiche ever is in balaunce,
"It stant not in my suffisaunce–."

Of Occleve's translation of Egidius *de Regimine principum*, not having it before me, I cannot transcribe the first lines. But here are the first that Mr. Warton has quoted from that poet, and he probably did not choose the worst. I should add, that Occleve wrote in the reign of King Henry V., about the year 1420:

"Aristotle, most famous philosofre,
"His epistles to Alisaunder sent,
"Whos sentence is wel bet then golde in cofre,
"And more holsum, grounded in trewe entent–"

The following is the first stanza of *the Letter of Cupide*, written by the same authour, and printed in Thynne's edition of Chaucer, 1561:

"Cupide, unto whose commaundement
"The gentill kinrede of goddes on hie
"And people infernall ben obedient,
"And al mortal folke serven busely,
"Of the goddesse sonne Cythera onely,
"To al tho that to our deite
"Ben subjectes, hertely greting sende we."

Of John Lydgate's *Historie of Troye*, which was finished about the year 1420, this is the beginning:

"O myghty Mars, that with thy sterne lyght
"In armys hast the power and the myght,
"And named arte from easte tyl occident
"The myghty lorde, the god armipotent,
"That with the shininge of thy stremes rede
"By influence dost the brydell lede
"Of chivalrie, as soveraygne and patron–."

The Hystorie of King Boccus and Sydracke, &c. printed in 1510, and written by Hugh Campeden in the reign of Henry VI. i.e.

some time between the year 1423 and 1461, begins thus:

"Men may finde in olde bookes,
"Who soo yat in them lookes,
"That men may mooche here,
"And yerefore yff yat yee wolle lere–."

Of Thomas Chestre's poems, entitled Sir Launfale, written about the same time, these are the first lines:

"Le douzty Artours dawes
"That held Engelond in good lawe,
"Ther fell a wondyr cas
"Of a ley that was ysette–."

The first lines that I have met with of Hardynge's *Chronicle of England unto the reign of king Edward the Fourth, in verse,* [composed about the year 1470, and printed in 1543, 4to] are as follows:

"Truly I heard Robert Ireliffee say,
"Clarke of the Greene Cloth, and that to the houshold
"Came every daye, forth must part alway,
"Ten thousand folke, by his messes told–."

The following is the only specimen that I have seen of *The Ordinal,* a poem written, by Thomas Norton, a native of Bristol, in the reign of King Edward IV.

"Wherefore he would set up in higth
"That bridge, for a wonderful sight,
"With pinnacles guilt, shinynge as goulde,
"A glorious thing for-men to behoulde."

The poem on *Hawking, Hunting, and Armoury,* written by

Julian Barnes in the reign of the same monarch, (about 1481,) begins thus:

"My dere sones, where ye fare, by frith, or by fell,
"Take good hede in this tyme, how Tristram woll teil,
"How many maner bestes of venery there were,
"Listenes now to our dame, and ye shullen here.",

The only extract that I have met with from William of Naffyngton's *Treatise on the Trinitie*, translated from John of Waldenby, about the year 1480, runs thus:

"I warne you first at the begynnynge,
"That I will make no vaine carpynge,
"Of dedes of armes, ne of amours,
"As does Mynstrellis and Gestours–."

I cannot adhere to the method that I have in general observed, by quoting the first lines of *the Moral Proverbes of Christyne* of Pyse, translated in metre by earl Rivers, and printed by Caxton in the seventeenth year of Edward IV. (1478), not having a copy of that scarce book. However, as this is the era of the pretended Rowley, I cannot forbear to transcribe the last stanza of that poem, as I find it cited in an account of this accomplished nobleman's works:

"Of these sayynges Christyne was the aucturesse,
"Which in makyn had such intelligence,
"That thereof she was mireur and maistresse;
"Her werkes testifie thexperience;
"In Frensh languaige was written this sentence;
"And thus englished doth hit reherse
"Antoin Widevylle therle Ryvers."

The first stanza of *the Holy Lyfe of Saynt Werburge*, written by Henry Bradshaw, about the year 1500, and printed in 1521, is this:

> "Whan Phebus had ronne his cours in sagittari,
> "And Capricorne entred a sygne retrograt,
> "Amyddes Decembre, the ayre colde and frosty,
> "And pale Lucyna the erthe dyd illuminat,
> "I rose up shortly fro my cubycle preparat,
> "Aboute mydnyght, and cast in myne intent,
> "How I myght spende the tyme convenyent."

Stephen Hawes's celebrated poem, entitled *the Passetyme of pleasure*, or the *Historie of Graunde Amour and La bell Pucell*, &c. (written about the year 1506, and printed by Wynkyn de Worde in 1517,) being now before me, I am enabled to transcribe the first lines:

> "When Phebus entred was in Geminy,
> "Shinyng above, in his fayre golden sphere,
> "And horned Dyane, then but one degre
> "In the crabbe had entred, fayre and cleare--."

Of the *Example of Virtue*[1], written by the same authour, and printed by Wynkyn de Worde in 1530, this is the first stanza:

> "In September, in fallynge of the lefe,
> "Whan Phebus made his inclynacyon,
> "And all the whete gadred was in the shefe,
> "By radyaunt hete and operacyon,
> "When the vyrgyn had full dominacyon,
> "And Dyane entred was one degre
> "Into the sygne of Gemyne–"

The first piece of Skelton, most of whose poems were written between 1509 and 1529, begins thus:

"Arrectynge my sight toward the zodiake
"The signes xii for to beholde a farre,
"When Mars retrogaunt reversed his backe,
"Lorde of the yere in his orbicular–."

The reader has now before him specimens of ancient poetry, during a period of near two hundred years; that is, for a century before the pretended Thomas Rowley is said to have written, and for near a century afterwards. They are for the most part taken from the commencement of the works of the several authours; so that there can be no suspicion of their having been selected, on account of their uncouthness, to prove a particular point. I know not whether I flatter myself; but by making these short extracts, I imagine that I have thrown more light upon the subject now under consideration, than if I had transcribed twenty pages of Junius, and as many of Skinner's *Etymologicon*, or Doomsday-book. Poetical readers may now decide the question for themselves; and I believe they will very speedily determine, that the lines which have been quoted from Chatterton's poems were not written at any one of the eras above mentioned, and will be clearly of opinion with Mr. Walpole, (whose unpublished pamphlet on this subject, printed at Strawberry Hill, shows him to be as amiable as he is lively and ingenious,) that this wonderful youth has indeed "copied ancient language, but ancient style he has never been able to imitate:" not for want of genius, for he was perhaps the second poetical genius that England has produced, but because he attempted something too arduous for human abilities to perform. My objection is not to single words, to lines or half-lines of these compositions (for here the advocates for their authenticity always shift their ground, and plead, that any particular exceptionable word or passage was the interpolation of Chatterton); but it is to their whole structure, style, and rythm. Many of the stones which this ingenious boy employed in his building, it must be acknowledged, are as old as those at Stone-henge; but the beautiful fabrick that he has raised

REMEMBERING THOMAS CHATTERTON

is tied together by modern cement, and is covered with a stucco of no older date than that of Mess. Wyat and Adams.

To be more particular: In what poet of the time of Edward IV., or for a century afterwards, will the Dean of Exeter find what we frequently meet with in the *Battle of Haftings* No1, and No2, at the conclusion of speeches–"*Thus be;*"–"*Thus Leofwine;*"–"*He said*; and as," &c? In none Iam confident. This latter is a form of expression in heroick poetry, that Pope has frequently made use of in his Homer (from whence Chatterton undoubtedly copied it), and was sometimes employed by Dryden and Cowley; but I believe it will not be easy to trace it to Harrington or Spenser; most assuredly it cannot be traced up to the fifteenth century.– In what English poem of that age will he find similies dressed in the modern garb with which Chatterton has clothed them throughout these pieces?–"*As when* a flight of cranes, &c.—*So prone*," &c.–"*As when* a drove of wolves, &c. *So* fought," &c. &c.– If the reverend Antiquarian can find this kind of phraseology in any one poet of the time of King Edward IV., or even for fifty years afterwards, I will acknowledge the antiquity of every line contained in his quarto volume. Most assuredly neither he nor his colleague can produce any such instance. Even in the latter end of the *sixteenth* century, (a large bound from 1460,) poetical comparisons, of the kind here alluded to, were *generally* expressed either thus–"*Look how* the crown that Ariadne wore, &c. *So*," &c. "*Look how* a comet at the first appearing, &c. *So* did the blazing of my blush," &c. "*Look how* the world's poor people are amazed, &c. *So*," &c.– Or thus: "*Even as* an empty eagle sharpe by fast, &c.–*Even so*," &c.–"*Like as* a taper burning in the darke, &c. *So*," &c.–Such is the general style of the latter end of the sixteenth century; though sometimes (but very rarely) the form that Chatterton has used was also employed by Spenser and others. In the preceding century, if I am not much mistaken, it was wholly unknown.

But I have perhaps dwelled too long on this point. Every poetical reader will find instances of modern phraseology in almost every page of these spurious productions. I will only add, before I quit the subject of style, that it is observable, that throughout these poems we never find a noun in the plural number joined with a verb in the singular; an offence against grammar which every ancient poet, from the time of Chaucer to that of Shakespeare, has frequently committed, and from which Rowley, if such a poet had existed, would certainly not have been exempted.

With respect to the stanza that Chatterton has employed in his two poems on the *Battle of Hastings*, Mr. Bryant and the Dean of Exeter seem to think that they stand on sure ground, and confidently quote Gascoigne, to prove that such a stanza was known to our old English poets. "The greatest part of Chaucer's Canterbury Tales (says the latter gentleman, p. 30), and his Legend of Good Women, are in the decasyllabick couplet; but *in general* Lidgate's, Occleve's, *Rowley's*, Spenser's, and a great part of Chaucer's poetry, is written in stanzas of *seven, eight,* or *nine* decasyllabick lines; *to which Rowley generally adds a tenth, and closes with an Alexandrine.* All these may be ranked under the title of Rithme Royal; of which Gascoigne, in his Instructions For English Verse, has given the following description: "Rithme Royal is a verse of ten syllables, and *seven* such verses make a stasse, whereof the sirst and third do answer acrosse in the terminations and rime; the second, fourth, and fifth, do likewise answer eche other in terminations; and the two last combine and shut up the sentence: this hath been called Rithme Royal, and surely it is a royal kind of verse, serving best for grave discourses." I leave it to the reverend Antiquarian to reconcile the contradictory assertions with which the passage I have now quoted sets out; and shall only observe, that we have here a great parade of authority, but nothing like a proof of the existence of such a stanza as Chatterton has used, in the time of K. Edward IV.; and at last the Commentator is obliged to have recourse to this flimzy kind of reasoning: "The different number of lines contained in the stanza makes no material alteration in the structure of this verse, the stanza always concluding with a couplet: in that of six lines, the four first rime alternately; in that of nine, wherein Spenser has composed his Fairy Queen, the sixth line rimes to the final couplet, and the seventh to the fifth: *Rowley having added another line to the stanza, the eighth rimes with the sixth.*"–The upshot of the whole is, that Rowley himself, or rather Chatterton, is at last the only authority to show that such a stanza was employed at the time mentioned. And it is just with this kind of circular proof that we are amused, when any very singular fact is mentioned in Chatterton's verses: "This fact, say the learned Commentators, is also minutely described by Rowley in the Yellow Roll, which wonderfully confirms the authenticity of these poems;" i.e. one forgery of Chatterton in prose, wonderfully supports and authenticates another forgery of his in rhyme.–To prevent the Dean from giving himself any farther trouble in searching for authorities to prove that the stanza of the *Battle of Hastings* (consisting of two quatrains rhyming alternately, and a couplet,) was known to our early writers, I beg leave to inform him, that it was not used till near three centuries after the time of the supposed Rowley; having been, if I remember right, first employed by Prior, who considered it as an improvement on that of Spenser.

II. The second point that I proposed to consider is, the imitations of Pope's Homer, Shakspeare, Dryden, Rowe, &c. with which these pieces abound. And here the cautious conduct of Chatterton's new commentator is very remarkable. All the similies that poor Chatterton borrowed from Pope's or Chapman's Homer, to embellish his *Battle of Hastings*, are exhibited boldly; but then "they were all clearly copied from the original of the Grecian Bard," in whom we are taught, that Rowley was better read than any other man, during the preceding or subsequent century: but in the tragedy of *Ella*, and other pieces, where we in almost every page meet with lines and half-lines of Shakspeare, Dryden, &c. the reverend Antiquarian is less liberal of his illustrations. Indeed when the fraud is so manifest as not to be concealed, the passage is produced. Thus in *Ella* we meet

> "My love is dead,
> "Gone to her death-bed,
> "All under the willow tree–"

and here we are told, "the burthen of this roundelay very much resembles that in Hamlet:"

> "And will he not come again?
> "And will he not come again?
> "No, no, he is dead;
> "Go to thy death-bed,
> "He never will come again."

But when we meet—"Why thou art all that pointelle can bewreen"–evidently from Rowe–"Is she not more than painting can exprefs?"–the editor is very prudently silent.

So also in the *Battle of Hastings* we find

> "In agonies and pain he then did lie,
> "While life and death strove for the mastery–"

clearly from Shakspeare:

> "That Death and Nature do contend about them,
> "Whether they live or die."

So also in *Ella*:

> "Fen-vapours blast thy every manly power!"

taken from the same author:

"As wicked *dew* as e'er my mother brushed
"With raven's feather from unwholesome *fen*,
"Light on you both!" [*Tempest.*]
"Ye *fen-suck'd fogs*, drawn by the powerful sun,
"To fall and *blast* &c." [*King Lear*]

Thus again in *Ella*:

"O thou, whate'er thy name, or Zabalus or Queede,
"Come steel my fable spright, for fremde and doleful
"deed–"

from the *Dunciad*:

"O thou, whatever title please thine ear,
"Dean, Drapier, &c."

But in all these, and twenty other places, not a word is said by the editor.–I am ashamed of taking up the time of my readers in discussing such points as these. Such plain and direct imitations as Chatterton's, could scarcely impose on a boy of fifteen at Westminster School.

In the *Battle of Hastings* we meet

"His noble soul came rushing from the wound–

from Dryden's Virgil–

"And the disdainsul soul came rushing through the wound–[2]"

and in Sir Charles Bawdin, "And tears began to flow;" Dryden's very words in *Alexander's Feast*. But it was hardly possible, says the learned Commentator, for these thoughts to be expressed in any other words. Indeed! I suppose five or six different modes of expressing the latter thought will occur to every reader.

Can it be believed, that every one of the lines I have now quoted, this gentleman maintains to have been written by a poet of the fifteenth century (for all that Chatterton ever did, according to his system, was supplying lacunæ, if there were any in the Mss., or modernizing a few antiquated phrases)? He argues indeed very rightly, that the *whole* of these poems must have been written by *one* person. "Two poets, (he observes) so distant in their æra [as Rowley and Chatterton], so different from each other in their age and disposition, could not have united their labours.[he *means*, their labours could not unite or coalesce] in the same poem to any effect, without such apparent difference in their style, language, and sentiments, as would have defeated Chatterton's intent of imposing his works on the public, as the original and entire composition of Rowley."–Most readers, I suppose, will more readily agree with his premises than his conclusion. Every part of these poems was undoubtedly writtten by one person; but that person was not Rowley, but Chatterton.

What reason have we to doubt, that he who imitated all the English poets with whom he was acquainted, likewise borrowed his Homerick images from the versions of Chapman and Pope; in the latter of which he found these allusions dressed out in all the splendid ornaments of the eighteenth century?

In the new commentary, indeed, on the *Battle of Hastings*, we are told again and again, that many of the similies which the poet has copied from Homer, contain circumstances that are found in the Greek, but omitted in Mr. Pope's translation. "Here therefore we have a certain proof that the authour of these poems could read Homer in the original[3]." But the youngest gownsman at Oxford or Cambridge will inform the reverend critick, that this is a *non sequitur*; for the poet might have had the assistance of *other* translations, besides those of Pope; the English prose version from that of Madame Dacier, the translations by Chapman and by Hobbes. Nor yet will it follow from his having *occasionally* consulted *these* versions, that he was *not at all indebted to Pope*; as this gentleman endeavours to persuade us. He availed himself, without doubt, of them all. Whenever the Commentator can show a single thought in these imitations of the Grecian Bard, that is found in the original, and not in *any* of those translations, I will readily acknowledge that *the Battle of Hastings*, and all the other pieces contained in his quarto volume, were written by Rowley, or Turgot, or Alfred the Great, or Merlin, or whatever other existent or non-existent ancient he or Mr. Bryant shall choose to ascribe them to. Most assuredly no such instance can be pointed out.

I do not however rest the matter here. What are we to conclude, if in Chattetton's imitations of Homer, we discover some circumstances that exist in Pope's translation, of which but very faint traces appear in the original Greek? Such, I believe, may be found. It is observable, that in all the similies we meet with many of the very rhymes that Pope has used. Will this Commentator contend, that the learned Rowley not only understood Homer, at a time when his contemporaries had scarcely heard of his name, but also foresaw in the reign of Edward IV. those additional graces with which Mr. Pope would embellish him three hundred years afterwards?

III. The Anachronisms come next under our consideration. Of these also the modern-antique compositions which we are now examining, afford a very plentiful supply; and not a little has been the labour of the reverend Commentator to do away their force. The sirst that I have happened to light upon is in the tragedy of *Ella*, p. 212:

> "She said, as her white hands white hosen were knitting,
> "What pleasure it is to be married!"

It is certain that the art of knitting stockings was unknown in the time of king Edward IV., the era of the pretended Rowley. This difficulty, therefore, was by all means to be gotten over. And whom of all men, think you, courteous reader, this sagacious editor has chosen as an authority to ascertain the high antiquity of this practice? No other than our great poet Shakspeare; who was born in 1564, and died in 1616. Poor Shakspeare, who gave to all the countries in the world, and to all preceding eras, the customs of his own age and country, he is the authour that is chosen for this purpose! "If this Scotch art (says the Commentator) was so far advanced in a foreign country in the beginning of the sixteenth century, can there be a doubt of its being known in England half a century earlier? At least the art of knitting, and weaving bone-lace, was *more ancient* than queen Elizabeth's time; for Shakspeare speaks of old and *antick* songs, which

> "The spinsters and the *knitters* in the fun,
> "And the free maids that *weave their thread with bone*,
> "Did use to chaunt."

Twelfth Night, Act II. Sc. 4.

It might be sussicient to observe, that the old songs which were chaunted by the spinsters and knitters of Shakspeare's days, do not veryclearly ascertain the antiquity of the *operation* on which they were employed; for I apprehend, though the art of knitting had not been invented till 1564, when the poet was born, the practisers of it might yet the very next day after it was known, sing ballads that were written a hundred years before.— In order, however, to give some colour to the forced inference that the commentator has endeavoured to extract from this passage, he has misquoted it; for Shakspeare does not say, as he has been represented, that the spinsters of old time *did* use to chaunt these songs: his words are,

> "O fellow, come, the song we had last night;
> "Mark it, Cesario, it is old and plain:
> "The spinsters and the knitters in the fun,

"And the free maids that weave their thread with bones,
"*Do* use to chaunt it."

These lines, it must be acknowledged, prove that the art was *as* old as the time of Shakspeare, but not one hour *more* ancient; nor would they answer the Commentator's purpose, even if they had been uttered by Portia in *Julius Cæsar,* by the Egyptian queen in *Antony and Cleopatra,* or by Nestor in *Troilus* and *Cressida*; for, as I have already observed, our great poet gave to all preceding times the customs of his own age.—If the learned editor should hereafter have occasion to prove, that *Dick* and *Hob* were common names at Rome, and that it was an usual practice of the populace there, two thousand years ago, to throw up their caps in the air, when they were merry, or wished to do honour to their leaders, I recommend the play of *Coriolanus* to his notice, where he will find proofs to this purpose, all equally satisfactory with that which he has produced from *Twelfth Night,* to show the antiquity of the art of knitting stockings in England.

Many of the poems and prose works attributed to Rowley, exhibit anachronisms similar to that now mentioned. Bristol is called a city, though it was not one till long after the death of king Edward IV. Cannynge is spoken of as possessing a *Cabinet* of coins and other curiosities[4], a century at least before any Englishman ever thought of forming such a collection. *Drawings,* in the modern and technical sense of delineations on paper or vellum, with chalks or Indian ink, are mentioned a hundred and fifty years before the word was ever used with that signification. *Manuscripts* are noticed as rarities, with the idea at present annexed to them; and eagerly sought after and purchased by Rowley, at a time when printed books were not known, and when all the literature of the times was to be found in manuscripts alone. All these anachronisms *decisively* prove the spuriousness of these compositions. Other anachronisms may be traced in the poems before us, but they are of less weight, being more properly poetical deviations from *costume.*

However I will briefly mention them. Tilts and tournaments are mentioned at a period when they were unknown. *God and my Right* is the word used by duke William in *the Battle of Hastings*, though it was first used by king Richard I. after the victory at Grizors; and hatchments and armorial bearings, which were first seen at the time of the Croisades, are introduced in other places with equal impropriety.

One of Chatterton's earliest fictions was an ode or short poem of two or three stanzas in *alternate rhyme*, on the death of that monarch, which he sent to Mr. Walpole, informing him at the same time, that it had been found at Bristol with many other ancient poems. This, however, either C. or his friends thought proper afterwards to suppress. It is not, I believe, generally known, that this is the era which was originally fixed upon by this wonderful youth for his forgeries, though afterwards, as appears from Mr. Walpole's pamphlet already mentioned, having been informed that no such metres as he exhibited as ancient, were known in the age of Richard I., he thought proper to shist the era of his productions. It is remarkable, that one line yet remains in these poems, evidently written on the first idea:

"Richard of lion's heart to sight *is* gone."

"It is very improbable, as the same gentleman observes, that Rowley, writing in the reign of Henry VI., or Edward IV., as is now pretended, or in that of Henry IV., as was assigned by the credulous, before they had digested their system, should incidentally, in a poem on another subject, say, *now is* Richard &c." Chatterton, having stored his mind with images and customs suited to the times he meant originally for the era of his fictitious ancient, introduced them as well as he could in subsequent compositions. One other singular circumstance, which I learn from the same very respectable authority, I cannot omit mentioning. Among the Mss. that Chatterton pretended to have discovered in the celebrated chest at Bristol was a painter's bill[5], of which, like the rest, he produced only a copy. Great was the triumph of his advocates. Here was an undoubted relick of antiquity! And so indeed it was; for it was faithfully copied from the first volume of the *Anecdotes of Painting*, printed some years before; and had been originally transcribed by Vertue from some old parchments in the church of St. Mary Redcliffe at Bristol (a person, by the by, who was indefatigable in the pursuit of everything that related to our ancient poets, and who certainly at the same time would have discovered some traces of the pretended Rowley, if any of his poetry had been lodged in that repository). Can there be a doubt, that he who was convicted of having forged this paper, and owned that he wrote the first *Battle of Hastings*, and the *Account of the ceremonies observed at the opening if the Old Bridge*, was the authour of all the rest also? Were he charged in a court of justice with having forged various notes, and clear evidence given of the fact, corroborated by the additional testimony of his having on a former occasion fabricated a Will of a very ancient date, would a jury hesitate to find him guilty, because two purblind old women should be brought into court, and swear that the Will urged against him had such an ancient appearance, the hand-writing and language by which the bequests were made was so old, and the parchment so yellow, that they could not but believe it to be a genuine deed of a preceding century?—But I have insensibly wandered from the subject of Anachronisms. So much, however, has been already said by others on this point, that I will now hasten to the last matter which I meant to consider, *viz.* the Mss. themselves, which are said to have contained these wonderful curiosities.

IV. And on this head we are told by Mr. B. that the hand-writing, indeed, is not that of any particular age, but that it is very difficult to know precisely the era of a Ms., especially when of great antiquity; that our kings wrote very different hands, and many of them such, that it is impossible to distinguish one from the other; and that the diminutive size of the parchments on which these poems were written, (of which, I think, the largest that these Commentators talk of is eight inches and a half long, and four and a half broad[6],) was owing to the great scarcity of parchment in former times, on which account the lines often appear in continuation, without regard to the termination of the verse.

Most of these assertions are mere *gratis dicta*, without any foundation in truth. I am not very well acquainted with the ancient Mss. of the fourteenth or fifteenth century: but I have now before me a very fair Ms. of the latter end of the sixteenth century, in which the characters are as regular and uniform as possible. If twenty Mss. were produced to me, some of that era, and others of eras prior and subsequent to it, I would undertake to point out the handwriting of the age of queen Elizabeth, which is that of the Ms. I speak of, from all the rest; and I make no doubt that persons who are conversant with the hand-writing of preceding centuries, could with equal precision ascertain the age of more ancient Mss. than any that I am possessed of. But the truth is, (as any one may see, who accurately examines the *facsimile* exhibited originally by Mr. Tyrwhitt in his edition of these poems, and now again by the Dean of Exeter in the new edition of them,) that Chatterton could not accurately and for any continuance, copy the hand-writing of the fifteenth century; nor do the Mss. that be produced exhibit the hand-writing of *any* century whatever. He had a turn for drawing and emblazoning; and he found, without doubt, some ancient deeds in his father's old chest. These he copied to the best of his power; but the hand-writing usually found in deeds is very different from the current hand-writing of the same age, and from that employed in transcribing poems. To copy even these deeds to any great extent, would have been dangerous, and have subjected him to detection. Hence it was, that he never produced any parchment so large as a leaf of common folio.—What we are told of the great scarcity of parchment formerly, is too ridiculous to be answered. Who has not seen the various beautiful Mss. of the works of Gower and Chaucer, in several publick and private libraries, on parchment and on vellum, a small part of any one of which would have been sussicient to contain all the poems of Rowley, in the manner in which they are pretended to have been written?—But any speculation on this point is but waste of time. If such a man as Rowley had existed, who could troul off whole verses of Shakspeare, Dryden, and Pope, in the middle of the fifteenth century, he would have had half the parchment in the kingdom at his command; statues would have been erected to him as the greatest prodigy that the world had ever seen; and in a few years afterwards, when printing came to be practised, the presses of Caxton and Wynkyn de Worde would have groaned with his productions.

Much stress is laid upon Chatterton's having been seen frequently writing, with old crumpled parchments before him. No doubt of the fact. How else could he have imitated old hands in *any* manner, or have been able to form even the few pretended originals that he did produce? But to whom did he ever show these old Mss. when he was transcribing them? To whom did he ever say—"Such and such characters denote such letters, and the verse that I now show you in this old parchment is of this import?" Whom did he call upon, knowing in ancient hands, (and such undoubtedly he might have found,) to establish, by the testimony of his own eyes, the antiquity, not of one, but of all these Mss? If an ingenuous youth (as Mr. W. justly observes), "enamoured of poetry, had really found a large quantity of old poems, what would he have done? Produced them cautiousy, and one by one, studied them, and copied their style, and exhibited sometimes a genuine, and sometimes a fictitious piece? or blazed the discovery abroad, and called in every lover of poetry and antiquity to participation of the treasure? The characters of imposture are on every part of the story; and were it true, it would still remain one of those improbable wonders, which we have no reason for believing." What has been said already concerning forged compositions, cannot be too often repeated. If these Mss. or any part of them exist, why are they not deposited in the British Museum, or some publick library, for the examination of the curious? Till they are produced, we have a right to use the language that Voltaire tells us was used to the Abbé Nodot. "Show us your Ms. of Petronius, which you say was found at Belgrade, or consent that nobody shall believe you. It is as salse that you have the genuine satire of Petronius in your hands, as it is false that that ancient satire was the work of a consul, and a picture of Nero's conduct. Desist from attempting to deceive the learned; you can only deceive the vulgar."

Beside the marks of forgery already pointed out, these poems bear yet another badge of fraud, which has not, I believe, been noticed by any critick. Chatterton's verses have been shown to be too smooth and harmonious to be genuine compositions of antiquity: they are liable at the same time to the very opposite objection, they are too old for the era to which they are ascribed. This sounds like a paradox; yet it will be found to be true. The versification is too modern; the language often too ancient. It is not the language of any particular period of antiquity, but of *two entire* centuries. This is easily accounted for. Chatterton had no other means of writing old language, but by applying to glossaries and dictionaries, and these comprise all the antiquated words of preceding times; many provincial words used perhaps by a northern poet, and entirely unknown to a southern inhabitant; many words also, used in a singular sense by our ancient bards, and perhaps by them only once. Chatterton drawing his stores from such a copious fource, his verses must necessarily contain words of various and widely-distant periods. It is highly probable, for this reason, that many of his lines would not have been understood by one who lived in the fifteenth century.— That the diction of these poems is often too obsolete for the era to which they are allotted[7], appears clearly from hence; many of them are much more difficult to a reader of this day, without a glossary, than anyone of the metrical compositions of the age of Edward IV. Let any person, who is not very profoundly skilled in the language of our elder poets, read a few pages of any of the

71

poems of the age of that king, from whence I have already given short extracts, without any glossary or assistance whatsoever; he will doubtless meet sometimes with words he does not understand, but he will find much fewer difficulties of this kind, than while he is perusing the poems attributed to Rowley. The language of the latter, without a perpetual comment, would in most places be unintelligible to a common reader. He might, indeed, from the context, *guess* at something like the meaning; but the lines, I am confident, will be found, on examination, to contain twenty times more obsolete and obscure words than any one poem of the age of king Edward IV, now extant.

Before I conclude, I cannot omit to take notice of two or three particulars on which the Dean of Exeter and Mr. Bryant much rely. The former, in his Dissertation on *Ella*, says, "Whatever claim might have been made in favour of Chatterton as the author [of *the Battle of Hastings*], founded either on his own unsupported and improbable assertion, or on the supposed possibility of his writing these two poems, assisted by Mr. Pope's translation [of Homer], no plea of this kind can be urged with regard to any other poem in the collection, and least of all to the dramatick works, or the tragedy of *Ella*; which required not only an elevation of poetic genius far superior to that possessed by Chatterton, but also such moral and mental qualifications as never entered into any part of his character or conduct, and which could not possibly be acquired by a youth of his age and inexperience." "Where (we are triumphantly asked) could he learn the nice rules of the Interlude, by the introduction of a chorus, and the application of their songs to the moral and virtuous object of the performance?"—Where?—from Mr. Mason's *Elfrida* and *Caractacus*, in which he found a perfect model of the Greek drama, and which doubtless he had read. But Ella "*inculcates the precepts of morality*;" and Chatterton, it is urged, was idle and dissolute, and therefore could not have been the authour of it. Has then the reverend editor never heard of instances of the purest system of morality being powerfully enforced from the pulpit by those who in their own lives have not been always found to adhere rigidly to the rules that they laid down for the conduct of others? Perhaps not; but I suppose many instances of this kind will occur to every reader. The world would be pure indeed, if speculative and practical morality were one and the same thing. "That knowledge of times, of men, and manners," without which, it is said, *Ella* could not have been written, I find no difficulty in believing to have been possessed by this very extraordinary youth. Did he not, when he came to London, instead of being dazzled and confounded by the various new objects that surrounded him, become in a short time, by that almost intuitive faculty which accompanies genius, so well acquainted with all the reigning topicks of discourse, with the manners and different pursuits of various classes of men, with the state of parties, &c. as to pour out from the press a multitude of compositions on almost every subject that could exercise the pen of the oldest and most experienced writer[8]? He who could do this, could compose the tragedy of Ella[9]: (a name, by the by, that he probably found in Dr. Percy's *Reliques of Ancient Poetry*, Vol. I. p. xxiv.)

Almost every part of the Dissertation on this tragedy is as open to observation as that now mentioned. It is not true, as is asserted, that the *rythmical tales*, before called *tragedies*, sirst assumed a regular dramatick form in the time of king Edward IV. These melancholy tales went under the name of tragedies for above a century afterwards. Many of the pieces of Drayton were called *tragedies* in the time of queen Elizabeth, though he is not known to have ever written a single drama. But without staying to point out all the mistakes of the reverend critick on this subject, I recommend to those readers who wish to form a decided opinion on these poems, the same test for the tragedy of *Ella* that I have already suggested for the *Battle of Hastings*. If they are not surnished with any of our dramatick pieces in the original editions, let them only cast their eyes on those ancient interludes which take up the greater part of Mr. Hawkins's first volume of *The Origin of the English Drama* (the earliest of them composed in 1512); and I believe they will not hesitate to pronounce *Ella* a modern composition. The dramas which are yet extant (if they can deserve that name), composed between the years 1540 and 1570, are such wretched stuff, that nothing but antiquarian curiosity can endure to read a page of them. Yet the period I speak of is near a century after the era of the pretended Rowley.

The argument of Mr. B. on this subject is too curious to be omitted: "I am sensible (says he, in his *Observations*, p. 166,) that the plays mentioned above [the Chester Mysteries] seem to have been confined to religious subjects.—But though the monks of the times confined themselves to these subjects, it does not follow that people of more learning and genius were limited in the same manner. As plays certainly existed, the plan might sometimes be varied; and the transition from sacred history to profane, was very natural and easy. Many generous attempts may have been made towards the improvement of the rude drama, and the introduction of compositions on a better model: but the ignorance of the monks, and the depraved taste of the times, may have prevented such writings being either countenanced or preserved. It may be said, that we have no examples of any compositions of this sort. But this is begging the question, *while we have the plays of Ælla and* Godwin *before us. The former is particularly transmitted to us as* Rowley's[10]." I believe no reader will be at a loss to determine, who it is that in this case *begs the question.* Here we have another remarkable instance of that kind of circular proof of which I have already taken notice.

In the multitude of topics agitated by these commentators, I had almost forgot one, much relied upon by the last-mentioned gentleman. It is the name of *Widdeville*, which, we are informed, (p. 317.) is written in all the old chronicles *Woodville*; and the question is triumphantly asked, "how could Chatterton, in his *Memoirs of Cannynge*, [*Miscell.* p. 119.] vary from all these chronicles?—Where could he have found the name of *Widdeville* except in one of those manuscripts to which we are so much beholden?" If the learned commentator's book should arrive at a second edition, I recommend it to him to cancel this page (as well as a former, in which he appears not to have known that "*happy* man *be his dole!*" is a common expression in Shakspeare, and for his ignorance of which he is forced to make an awkward apology in his Appendix); and beg leave to inform him, that Chatterton found the name of *Widdeville* in a very modern, though now scarce, book, the *Catalogue of the Royal and Noble Authors of England*[11], by Mr. Walpole, every one of whose works most assuredly Chatterton had read.

The names of the combatants in *the Battle of Hastings*, an enumeration of which takes up one third of this commentator's work, and which, he tells us, are only to be found in Doomsdaybook and other ancient records that Chatterton could not have seen, have been already shown by others to be almost all mentioned in Fox's *Book of Martyrs*, and the *Chronicles* of Holinshed and Stowe. And what difficulty is there in supposing that the names not mentioned in any printed work (if any such there are) were found in the old deeds that he undoubtedly examined, and which were more likely to furnish him with a catalogue of names than any other ancient muniment whatsoever? It is highly probable also, that in the same chest which contained these deeds, he found some old Diary of events relating to Bristol, written by a mayor or alderman of the fifteenth century, that furnished him with some account of Rowley and Cannynge, and with those circumstances which the commentators say are only to traced in William de Wircester. The practice of keeping diaries was at that time very general, and continued to be much in use to the middle of the last century. This, it must be owned, is a mere hypothesis, but by no means an improbable one.

I cannot dismiss this gentleman without taking notice of a position which he has laid down, and is indeed the basis of almost all the arguments that he has urged to prove the authenticity of the Bristol Mss. It is this; that as every authour must know his own meaning, and as Chatterton has sometimes given wrong interpretations of words that are found in the poems attributed to Rowley, he could not be the authour of those poems.

If Chatterton had originally written these poems, in the form in which they now appear, this argument might in a doubtful question have some weight. But although I have as high an opinion of his abilities as perhaps any person whatsoever, and do indeed believe him to have been the greatest genius that England has produced since the days of Shakspeare, I am not ready to acknowledge that he was endued with any miraculous powers. Devoted as he was from his infancy to the study of antiquities, he could not have been so conversant with ancient language, or have had all the words necessary to be used so present to his mind, as to write antiquated poetry of any considerable length, off hand. He, without doubt, wrote his verses in plain English, and afterwards embroidered them with such old words as would suit the sense and metre. With these he furnished himself, sometimes probably from memory, and sometimes from glossaries; and annexed such interpretations as he found or made. When he could not readily find a word that would suit his metre, he invented one[12] If then his old words afford some sense, and yet are sometimes interpreted wrong, nothing more follows than that his glossaries were imperfect, or his knowledge inaccurate; (still however he might have had a confused, though not complete, idea of their import:) if, as the commentator asserts, the words that he has explained not only suit the places in which they stand, but are often more apposite than he imagined, and have a latent and significant meaning, that never occurred to him, this will only show, that a man's book is sometimes wiser than himself; a truth of which we have every day so many striking instances, that it was scarcely necessary for this learned antiquarian to have exhibited a new proof of it.

Let it be considered too, that the glossary and the text were not always written at the same time; that Chatterton might not always remember the precise sense in which he had used antiquated words; and from a confused recollection, or from the want of the very same books that he had consulted while he was writing his poems, might add sometimes a false, and sometimes an imperfect, interpretation.—This is not a mere hypothesis; for in one instance we know that the comment was written at some interval of time after the text. "The glossary of the poem entitled *the Englysh Metamorposis* (Mr. Tyrwhitt informs us) was written down by C. extemporally, without the assistance of any book, at the desire and in the presence of Mr. Barrett."

I have here given this objection all the sorce that it can claim, and more perhaps than it deserves; for I doubt much whether in Chatterton's whole volume six instances can be pointed out, where he has annexed false interpretations to words that appear when rightly understood to suit the context, and to convey a clear meaning: and these mistakes, if even there are so many as have been mentioned, are very easily accounted for from the causes now assigned.

Perhaps it may be urged, that when I talk of the manner in which these poems were composed, I am mysels guilty of the fault with which I have charged others, that of assuming the very point in controversy; and the observation would be just, if there were not many collateral and decisive circumstances, by which Chatterton is clearly proved to have written them. All these concurring to show that he forged these pieces, an investigation of the *manner* in which he forged them, cannot by any fair reasoning be construed into an assumption of the question in dispute.

Great stress is also laid by this commentator on some variations being found in the copies of these poems that were produced by Chatterton at different times; or, to use his own words, "there is often a material variation between the copy and the original, which never could have happened if he had been the author of both[13]. He must have known his own writing, and would not have deviated from his own purpose."—Thus in one copy of *the Song to Ella*, which C. gave to Mr. Barrett, these lines were found:

> "or seest the hatched steed,
> "*Ifrayning* o'er the mead."

Being called upon for the original, he the next day produced a parchment, containing the same poem, in which he had written *yprauncing*, instead of *ifrayning*; but by some artifice he had obscured the Ms. so much, to give it an ancient appearance, that Mr. B. could not make out the word without the use of galls.—What follows from all this, but that C. found on examination that there was no such word as *ifrayning*, and that he substituted another in its place? In the same poem he at one time wrote *locks—burlie—brasting*—and *kennest*; at another, *hairs—valiant—bursting*—and *hearest*. Variations of this kind he could have produced without end.—These commentators deceive themselves, and use a language that for a moment may deceive others, by talking of one reading being found in the *copy*, and another in the *original*, when in fact all the Mss. that C. produced were equally originals. What he called originals indeed, were probably in general more perfect than what he called copies; because the former were always produced after the other, and were in truth nothing more than second editions of the same pieces[14].

The inequality of the poems which Chatterton owned as his own compositions, when compared with those ascribed to Rowley, has been much insisted upon. But this matter has been greatly exaggerated. Some of the worst lines in Chatterton's *Miscellanies* have been selected by Mr. Bryant to prove the point contended for; but in fact they contain the same even and flowing versification as the others, and in general display the same premature abilities[15].—The truth is, the readers of these pieces are deceived insensibly on this subject. While they are perusing the poems of the fictitious Rowley, they constantly compare them with the poetry of the fifteenth century; and are ready every moment to exclaim, how much he surpasses all his contemporaries. While the verses that Chatterton acknowledged as his own, are passing under their eyes, they still recollect that they are the productions of a boy of seventeen; and are slow to allow them even that merit which they undoubtedly possess. "They are ingenious, but puerile; flowing, but not sufficiently correct."—The best way of convincing the antiquarian reader of the merit of these compositions, would be to disfigure them with old spelling; as perhaps the most complete confutation of the advocates for the authenticity of what are called Rowley's poems would be to exhibit an edition of them in modern orthography.— Let us only apply this very simple test,—"handy-dandy let them change places," and I believe it would puzzle even the President of the Society of Antiquaries himself to determine, "which is the justice, and which is the thief;" which is the pretended ancient, and which the acknowledged modern.

Of this double transformation I subjoin a short specimen; which is not selected on account of any extraordinary spirit in the lines that precede, or uncommon harmony in those that follow, but chosen (agreeably to the rule that has been observed in all the former quotations) merely because the *African Eclogue* happens to be the *first* poetical piece inserted in Chatterton's acknowledged *Miscellanies*.

I. CHATTERTON *in Masquerade.*
NARVA AND MORED: AN AFRICAN ECLOGUE

[From Chatterton's *Miscellanies*, p. 56.]

"Recyte the loves of Narva and Mored,
"The preeste of Chalmas trypell ydolle sayde.
"Hie fro the grounde the youthful heretogs sprunge,
"Loude on the concave shelle the launces runge:

79

"In al the mysterke maizes of the daunce
"The youths of Bannies brennynge sandes advaunce;
"Whiles the mole vyrgin brokkyng lookes behinde,
"And rydes uponne the penyons of the winde;
"Astighes the mountaines borne and meafures rounde
"The sleepie clifftes of Chalmas hallie grounde."

II. CHATTERTON UNMASKED.
ECLOGUE THE FIRST

[From Rowley's Poems, quarto, p. 391.]

"When England smoking from her deadly wound,
"From her gall'd neck did twitch the chain away,
"Seeing her lawful sons fall all around,
"(Mighty they fell, 'twas Honour led the fray,)
"Then in a dale, by eve's dark surcoat gray,
"Two lonely shepherds did abruptly fly,

"(The rustling leaf does their white hearts affray,)
"And with the owlet trembled and did cry:
"First Robert Neatherd his sore bosom struck,
"Then fell upon the ground, and thus he spoke."

If however, after all, a little inferiority should be found in Chatterton's acknowledged productions, it may be easily accounted for. Enjoin a young poet to write verses on any subject, and after he has finished his exercise, show him how Shakspeare, Dryden, and Pope, have treated the same subject. Let him then write a second copy of verses, still on the same theme. This latter will probably be a Cento from the works of the authours that he has just perused. The one will have the merit of originality; the other a finer polish and more glowing imagery. This is exactly Chatterton's case. The verses that he wrote for Rowley are perhaps better than his others, because they contain the thoughts of our best poets often in their own words. The versification is equally good in both. Let it be remembered too, that the former were composed at his leisure in a period of near a year and a half; the latter in about four months, and many of them to gain bread for the day that was passing over him.

After his arrival in London, if his forgeries had met with any success, he would undoubtedly have produced ancient poetry without end; but perceiving that the gentleman in whom he expected to find at once a dupe and a patron, was too clearsighted to be deceived by such evident fictions, and that he could earn a livelihood by his talents, without fabricating old Mss. in order to gain a few shillings from Mess. Barrett and Catcott, he deferred his original plan, and we hear little more of Rowley's verses.

With regard to the time in which the poems attributed to this priest were produced, which it is urged was much too short for Chatterton to have been the inventor of them, it is indeed astonishing that this youth should have been able to compose, in about eighteen months, three thousand seven hundred verses, on various subjects; but it would have been still more astonishing, if he had transcribed in that time the same number of lines, written on parchment, in a very ancient hand, in the close and indistinct manner, in which these poems are pretended to have been written, and defaced and obliterated in many places[16]:— unless he had been endued with the faculty of a celebrated solicitor, who being desired a few years ago in the House of Lords to read an old deed, excused himself by saying that it was illegible, informing their lordships at the same time that he would make out a fair copy of it against the next day. Chatterton, I believe, understood better how to make fair copies of illegible parchments, than to read any ancient manuscript whatsoever.

It is amusing enough to observe the miseraeble shifts to which his new editor is forced to have recourse, when he is obliged to run full tilt against matters of fact.—Thus Chatterton, we find, owned that he was the authour of the first Battle of Hastings; but we are not to believe his declaration, says Mr. Thistlethwaite, whose doctrine on this subject the reverend commentator has adopted. "Chatterton thought himself not sufficiently rewarded by his Bristol patrons, in proportion to what his communications deserved." He pretended, therefore, "on Mr. Barrett's repeated solicitations for the original [of the Battle of Hastings], that he himself wrote that poem for a friend; thinking, perhaps, that if he parted with the original poem, he might not be properly rewarded for the loss of it.[17]"—As if there was no other way for him to avoid being deprived of a valuable ancient Ms. but by saying that it was a forgery, and that he wrote it himself!—What, however, did he do immediately afterwards? No doubt, he avoided getting into the same difficulty a second time, and subjecting himself again to the same importunity from his ungenerous Bristol patrons, by showing them no more of these rarities? Nothing less. The very same day that he acknowledged this forgery, he informed Mr. Barrett that he had another poem, the copy of an original by Rowley; and at a considerable interval of time (which indeed was requisite for writing his new piece) he produced another Battle of Hastings, much longer than the former; a fair copy from an undoubted original.—He was again, without doubt, pressed by Mr. B. to show the original Ms. of this also; and, according to Mr. Thistlethwaite's system, he ought again to have asserted that this poem likewise was a forgery; and so afterwards of every copy that he produced.—Can any person that considers this transaction for a moment entertain a doubt that all these poems were his own invention?

Again:—We have the positive testimony of Mr. John Ruddall, a native and inhabitant of Bristol, who was well acquainted with Chatterton, when he was a clerk to Mr. Lambert, that the Account of the ceremonies observed at the opening of the Old Bridge, published in Farley's Journal, Oct. I. 1768, and said to be taken from an ancient Ms., was a forgery of Chatterton's, and acknowledged by him to be such. Mr. Ruddall's account of this transaction is so material, that I will transcribe it from the Dean of Exeter's new work, which perhaps many of my readers may not have seen:—"During that time, [while C. was clerk to Mr. L.] Chatterton frequently called upon him at his master's house, and soon after he had printed the account of the bridge in the Bristol paper, told Mr. Ruddall, that he was the author of it; but it occurring to him afterwards, that he might be called upon to produce the original, he brought to him one day a piece of parchment about the size of a half-sheet of fool's-cap paper: Mr. Ruddall does not think that anything was written on it when produced by Chatterton, but he saw him write several words, if not lines, in a character which Mr. Ruddall did not understand, which he says was totally unlike English, and as he apprehends was meant by Chatterton to imitate or represent the original from which this account was printed. He cannot determine precisely how much Chatterton wrote in this manner, but says, that the time he spent in that visit did not exceed three quarters of an hour: the size of the parchment, however, (even supposing it to have been filled with writing) will in some measure ascertain the quantity which it contained. He says also, that when Chatterton had written on the parchment, he held it over the candle, to give it the appearance of antiquity, which changed the colour of the ink, and made the parchment appear black and a little contracted[18]." Such is the account of one of Chatterton's intimate friends. And how is this decisive proof of his abilities to imitate ancient English handwriting, and his exercise of those abilities, evaded? Why truly, we are told, "the contraction of the parchment is no discriminating mark of antiquity; the blackness given by smoke appears upon trial to be very different from the yellow tinge which parchment acquires by age; the ink does not change its colour, as Mr. Ruddall seems to apprehend." So, because these arts are not always completely successfull, and would not deceive a very skilful antiquary, we are to conclude, that Chattetton did not forge a paper which he acknowledged to have forged, and did not in the presence of Mr. Ruddall cover a piece of parchment with ancient characters for the purpose of imposition, though the

fact is clearly ascertained by the testimony of that gentleman!—
The reverend Commentator argues on this occasion much
in the same manner, as a well-known versifier of the present
century, the facetious Ned Ward (and he too published a quarto
volume of poems). Some biographer, in an account of the lives
of the English poets, had said that "he was an ingenious writer,
considering his low birth and mode of life, he having for some
time kept a publick house in the City." "Never was a greater or
more impudent calumny (replied the provoked rhymer); it is
very well known to every body, that my publick house is not in
the City, but in Moorfields."—In the name of common sense, of
what consequence is it, whether in fact all ancient parchments
are shrivelled; whether smoke will give ink a yellow appearance
or not. It is sufficient, that Chatterton thought this was the case;
that he made the attempt in the presence of a credible witness, to
whom he acknowledged the purpose for which the manoeuvre
was done. We are, asked indeed, why he did not prepare his
pretended original before he published the copy. To this another
question is the best answer. Why is not fraud always uniform
and consistent, and armed at all points? Happily for mankind it
scarcely ever is. Perhaps (as Mr. Ruddall's account seems to state
the matter) he did not think at first that he should be called upon
for the original: perhaps he was limited in a point of time, and
could not fabricate it by the day that the new bridge was opened
at Bristol.—But there is no end of such speculations. Facts are
clear and incontrovertible. Whatever might have been the cause
of his delay, it is not denied that he acknowledged this forgery to
his friend Mr. Ruddall; conjuring him at the same time not to
reveal the secret imparted to him. If this had been a mere frolick,
what need of this earnest injunction of secrecy?—His friend
scrupulously kept his word till the year 1779, when, as the Dean
of Exeter informs us, "on the prospect of procuring a gratuity
of ten pounds for Chatterton's mother, from a gentleman who
sought for information concerning her son's history, he thought
so material a benefit to the family would fully justify him for

divulging a secret, by which no person living could be a sufferer."

I will not stay to take notice of the impotent attempts that Chatterton's new commentators have made to overturn the very satisfactory and conclusive reasoning of Mr. Tyrwhitt's Appendix to the former edition of the fictitious Rowley's Poems. That most learned and judicious critick wants not the assistance of my feeble pen: *Non tali auxilio, nec defensoribus istis*—. If he should come into the field himself (as I hope he will), he will soon silence the Anglo-Saxon batteries of his opponents.

The principal arguments that have been urged in support of the antiquity of the poems attributed to Rowley, have now, if I mistake not, been fairly stated and examined[19]. On a review of the whole, I trust the reader will agree with me in opinion, that there is not the smallest reason for believing a single line of them to have been written by any other person than Thomas Chatterton; and that, instead of the towering motto which has been affixed to the new and splendid edition of the works of that most ingenious—Renascentur quæ, iam cecidere—the words of Claudian would have been more "germane to the matter:"

—tolluntur in altum,
Ut lapsu graviore ruant.

Having, I fear, trespassed too long on the patience of my readers, in the discussion of a question that to many may appear of no great importance, I will only add the following serious and well-intended propofal. I do humbly recommend, that a committee of the friends of the reverend antiquarian, Dr. Jeremiah Milles, Dean of Exeter, and the learned mythologist, Jacob Bryant, Esq., may immediately meet;—that they may, as soon as possible, convey the said Dr. M. and Mr. B. together with Mr. George Catcott, pewterer, and Mr. William Barrett, surgeon, of Bristol, and Dr. Glynn of Cambridge, to the room over the north porch of Redcliffe church, and that on the door of the said room six padlocks may be fixed:—that in order to wean thefe gentlemen by degrees from the delusion under which they labour, and to furnish them with some amusement, they may be supplied with proper instruments to measure the length, breadth, and depth, of the empty chests now in the said room, and thereby to ascertain how many thousand diminutive pieces of parchment, all eight inches and a half by four and a half, might have been contained in those chests; [according to my calculation, 1,464,578;—but I cannot pretend to be exact:] that for the sustenance of these gentlemen, a large peck loaf may be placed in a maund basket in the said room, having been previously prepared and left in a damp place, so as to become mouldy, and the words and figures Thomas Flour, Bristol, 1769, being first impressed in common letters on the upper crust of the said loaf, and on the under side thereof, in Gothick Characters, Thomas Wheateley, 1464 (which Thomas Wheateley Mr. Barrett, if he carefully examines Rowley's Purple Roll[20], will find was an auncyent baker, and "did use to bake daiely for Maister Canynge twelve manchettes of chete breade, and foure douzenne of marchpanes;" and which custom of impressing the names of bakers upon bread, I can prove to be as ancient as the time of king Edward IV., from Doomsday-book, William de Wircestre, Shakspeare, and other good antiquarians, as also from the Green and Yellow Rolls, now in Mr. B's custody) [21]:—that a proper quantity of water may be conveyed into the forementioned room in one of Mr. Catcott's deepest and most ancient pewter plates, together with an ewer of Wedgwood's ware, made after the oldest and most uncouth pattern that has yet been discovered at Herculaneum;—that Dr. Glynn, if he shall be thought to be sufficiently composed (of which great doubts are entertained), be appointed to cut a certain portion of the said bread for the daily food of these gentlemen and himself; and that, in order to sooth in some measure their unhappy fancies, he may be requested, in cutting the said loaf, to use the valuable knife of Mr. Shiercliffe (now in the custody of the said Dr. G), the history[22] of which has so much illustrated, and so clearly evinced the antiquity of the poems attributed to Thomas Rowley. And if in a fortnight after these gentlemen have been so confined, they shall be found to be entirely re-established in their health, and perfectly composed, I recommend that the six locks may be struck off, and that they all may be suffered to return again to their usual employments.

FIRST PUBLISHED IN 1781

FOOTNOTES

[1] This very rare poem escaped the researches of the learned and ingenious Mr. Warton, who doubted whether it had ever been printed. See his Hist. of Eng. Poetry, vol.II p. 211.

[2] It is observable, that this is the last line of the translation of the Æneid.

[3] To show how very weak and inconclusive the arguments of Chatterton's new Editor are on this head, I shall cite but one passage, from which the reader may form a judgment of all the other illustrations with which he has decorated the Battle of Hastings:

"Siere de Broque an arrowe longe lett flie,
"Intending Herewaldus to have sleyne;
"It miss'd, but hytte Edardus on the eye,
"And at his pole came out with horrid payne."

So Homer (says the Commentator):

ὀϊςὸν ἀπὸ νευρῆφιν ἴαλλεν
Ἕκτορος ἀντικρὺ, βαλέειν δὲ ἑ ἵετο θυμός·

87

καὶ μέν ῥ ἀφάμαρθ᾽ ὁ δ᾽ ἀμύμονα Γοργυθίωνα
Υἱὸν ἐῢν Πριάμοιο, κατὰ ϛτῆθος βάλεν ἰῷ

Il. Θ. v. 300.

"He said, and twang'd the string, the weapon flies
"At Hector's breast, and sings along the skies;
"He mifs'd the mark, but piere'd Gorgythio's heart."

Pope, B. viii. v. 365.

"The imitation here seems to be very apparent, but it is the imitation of Homer, and not of Pope; both Homer and Rowley express the intention of the archer, which is dropped by the translator of the Greek poet." Chatterton's Poems, quarto, p. 83. Edit. Milles. To my apprehension, the intention of the archer is very clearly expressed in Pope's lines; but it is unnecessary to contest that point, for lo! thus has old Chapman translated the same passage:

"This said, another arrow forth from his stiffe string he sent
"At Hector, whom he long'd to wound; but still amisse it went;
"His shaft smit faire Gorgythion."

Of such reasoning is the new Commentary on Chatterton's poems composed.

[4] Chatterton in his description of Cannynge's love of the arts, &c. seems often to have had Mr. Walpole in his eye; which was very natural, that gentleman being probably the first person who was at once a man of literature and rank, of whose character he had any knowledge—Thus, Mr. W. having a very curious collection of pictures, prints, &c. Cannynge too must be furnished with a cabinet of coins and other rarities; and there being a private printing-press at Strawberry-Hill, (the only one perhaps in

88

England,) the Bristol Mayor must likewise have one. It is in one of his letters that has not yet been printed, that Chatterton mentions his having read an account in the Rowley Mss. of Cannynge's intention to set up a printing-press at Westbury! This merchant died in 1474; during the greater part of his life printing was unknown; and even at the time of his death there was but one printing-press in this kingdom, namely, that set up by Caxton, in the Almonry of Westminster Abbey, about the year 1471.

[5] This fraud having been detected, we hear no more of it; but in the room of it has been substituted A List of skyllde Payneterrs and Carvellers, which is now said to have been found along with the other Mss. and to be in the possession of Mr. Barret, of Bristol.

[6] At the bottom of each sheet of old deeds (of which there were many in the Bristol chest) there is usually a blank space of about four or five inches in breadth. C. therefore found these slips of discoloured parchment at hand.

[7] Mr. Bryant seems to have been aware of this objection, and thus endeavours to obviate it. "Indeed in some places the language seems more obsolete than could be expected for the time of king Edward the Fourth; and the reason is, that some of the poems, however new modelled, were prior to that æra. For Rowley himself [i.e. Chatterton] tells us that he borrowed from Turgot; and we have reason to think that he likewise copied from Chedder." This same Chedder, he acquaints us in a note, was "a poet mentioned in the Mss., [that is, in Chatterton's Mss., for I believe his name is not to be found elsewhere.] who is supposed to have flourished about the year 1330. He is said [by Chatterton] to have had some maumeries at the comitating the city." Observations, p. 553.

I wonder the learned commentator did not likewise inform

us, from the same unqestionable authority, what wight Maistre Chedder copied.

[8] The following notices, which Mr. Walpole has preserved, are too curious to be omitted. They will give the reader a full idea of the professed authorship of Chatterton. In a list of pieces written by him, but never published, are the following: 5. "To Lord North. A Letter signed the Moderator, and dated May 26, 1770, beginning thus: "My Lord—It gives me a painful pleasure, &c.—This (says Mr. W.) is an encomium on administration for rejecting the Lord Mayor Beckford's Remonstrance. 6. A Letter to Lord Mayor Beckford, signed Probus, dated May 26, 1770.—This is a violent abuse of Government for rejecting the Remonstrance, and begins thus: "When the endeavours of a spirited people to free themselves from an insupportable slavery"—. On the back of this essay, which is directed to Chatterton's friend, Cary, is this indorsement: "Accepted by Bingley—set for and thrown out of The North Briton, 21 June, on account of the Lord Mayor's death.

[9] Chatterton wrote also "a Manks Tragedy," which, if his forgeries had met with a more favourable reception than they did, he would doubtless have produced as an ancient composition. With the ardour of true genius, he wandered to the untrodden paths of the little Isle of Man for a subject, and aspired

> petere inde coronam,
> Unde prius nulli velarint tempora Musæ.

[10] In the same manner argues the learned pewterer of Bristol, Mr. George Catcott. "These poems are certainly genuine, "for Rowley himself mentions them in the Yellow Roll." See his letter in the Gentleman's Magazine, vol. XLVIII. p. 348.

[11] See the first volume of that entertaining work, p. 67; art. Antony Widville, Earl Rivers.

[12] In Chatterton's poems many words occur, that were undoubtedly coined by him; as mole, dolce, droke, glytted, aluste, &c. All these his new editor has inserted in a very curious performance which he is pleased to call a Glossary, with such interpretations as as the context supplied, without even attempting to support them either by analogy or the authority of our ancient writers.

[13] So that an authour cannot revise or correct his works without forfeiting his title to them!—According to this doctrine, Garth was the authour of only the first copy of the the Dispensary, and all the subsequent editions published in his life-time, in every one of which there were material variations, must be attributed to some other hand.

[14] "Bie," which he wrote inadvertently in the tragedy of Ella, instead of "mie," (on which Mr. B. has given us a learned dissertation)—"Bie thankes I ever onne you wylle bestowe"—is such a mistake as every man in the hurry of writing is subject to. By had probably occurred just before, or was to begin some subsequent line that he was then forming in his mind. Even the slow and laborious Mr. Capel, who was employed near forty years in preparing and printing an edition of Shakspeare, in a Catalogue which he presented to a publick library at Cambridge, and which he probably had revised for many months before he gave it out of his hands, has written "Bloody Bloody," as the title of one of Fletcher's Plays, instead of "Bloody Brother."

[15] The observations on this subject, of the ingenious authour of the accurate account of Chatterton, in a book entituled Love and Madness, are too pertinent to be here omitted. "It may be asked why Chatterton's own Miscellanies are inferior to Rowley? Let me ask another question: Are they inferior? Genius, abilities, we may bring into the world with us; these rare ingredients may be mixed up in our compositions by the hand of Nature. But Nature herself

91

cannot create a human being possessed of a complete knowledge of our world almost the moment he is born into it. Is the knowledge of the world which his Miscellanies contain, no proof of his astonishing quickness in seizing every thing he chose? Is it remembered when, and at what age, Chatterton for the sirst time quitted Bristol, and how few weeks he lived afterwards? Chatterton's Letters and Miscellanies, and every thing which the warmest advocate for Rowley will not deny to have been Chatterton's, exhibit an insight into men, manners, and things, for the want of which, in their writings, authors who have died old men, with more opportunities to know the world, (who could have less than Chatterton?) have been thought to make amends by other merits."—"In London (as the same writer observes) was to be learned that which even genius cannot teach, the knowledge of life. Extemporaneous bread was to be earned more suddenly than even Chatterton could write poems for Rowley; and, in consequence of his employments, as he tells his mother, publick places were to be visited, and mankind to be frequented."— Hence, after "he left Bristol, we see but one more of Rowley's poems, The Ballad of Charitie, and that a very short one."

[16] Let those who may be surprised at this assertion, recollect the wonderful inventive faculties of Chatterton, and the various compositions, both in prose and verse, which he produced after his arrival in London, in the short space of four months; not to mention the numerous pieces, which he is known to have written in the same period, and which have not yet been collected— Let them likewise examine any one of the defaced Mss. of the fifteenth century, in the Cotton Library, and see in what time they can transcribe a dozen lines from it.

[17] Chatterton's Poems, quarto, edit. Milles, p. 458. It was not without good reason that the editor was solicitous to disprove Chatterton's frank confession, respecting this poem; for he perceived clearly that the style, the colouring, and images, are

nearly the same in this, and the second poem with the same title, and that every reader of any discernment must see at the first glance, that he who wrote the first Battle of Hastings was the authour of all the other poems ascribed to Rowley.—It is observable that Chatterton in the Battle of Hastings, No 2, frequently imitates himself, or repeats the same images a second time. Thus in the first poem with this title we meet

—"he dying gryp'd the recer's limbe;
"The recer then beganne to flynge and kicke,
"And toste the erlie farr off to the grounde:
"The erlie's squier then a swerde did flicke
"Into his harte, a dedlie ghastlie wounde;
"And downe he felle upon the crymson pleine,
"Upon Chatillion's soulless corse of claie."

In the second Battle of Hastings are these lines:

"But as he drewe his bowe devoid of arte,
"So it came down upon Troyvillain's horse;
"Deep thro hys hatchments wente the pointed floe;
"Now here, now there, with rage bleedinge he rounde doth goe.
"Nor does he hede his mastres known commands,
"Tyll, growen furiouse by his bloudie wounde,
"Erect upon his hynder feete he staundes,
"And throwes hys mastre far off to the grounde.

Can any one for a moment doubt that these verses were all written by the same person?—The circumstance of the wounded horse's falling on his rider, in the first of these similies, is taken directly from Dryden's Virgil, Æn. X. v. 1283.—Chatterton's new editor has artfully contrasted this passage of Dryden with the second simile, where that circumstance is not mentioned.

[18] See the new edition of Chatterton's poems, quarto, p. 436, 437.

[19] I take this opportunity of acknowledging an error into which
I have fallen in a former page, where it is said, that no instances
are found in these poems of a noun in the plural number being
joined to a verb in the singular. On a more careful examination
I observe that C. was aware of this mark of antiquity, and that
his works exhibit a few examples of this disregard to grammar.
He has however sprinkled them too sparingly. Had these poems
been written in the fifteenth century, Priscian's head would
have been broken in almost every page, and I should not have
searched for these grammatical inaccuracies in vain.

[20] Rowley's Purple Roll, Mr. Bryant very gravely tells us, is yet
extant in manuscript in his own hand-writing. "It is (he adds) in
two parts; one of the said parts written by Thomas Rowley, and
the other by Thomas Chatterton."

[21] A learned friend, who, by the favour of Mr. Barrett, has perused
the Yellow Roll, informs me, that Rowley, in a treatise dated 1451,
and addressed "to the dygne Maister Canynge," with the quaint
title, De re frumentaria, (chap. XIII. Concernynge Horse-hoeing
Husbandrie, and the Dryll-Ploughe) has this remarkable passage:
"Me thynketh ytt were a prettie devyce yffe this practyce of oure
bakerres were extended further. I mervaile moche, our seriveynes
and amanueses doe not gette lytel letters cutt in wood, or caste
in yron, and thanne followynge by the eye, or with a fescue,
everyche letter of the boke thei meane to copie, fix the sayde
wooden or yron letters meetelie disposed in a frame or chase;
thanne daube the same over with somme atramentous stuffe,
and layinge a thynne piece of moistened parchment or paper on
these letters, presse it doune with somme smoothe stone or other
heavie weight: by the whiche goodlye devyce a manie hundreth
copies of eche boke might be wroughte off in a few daies, insteade
of employing the eyen and hondes of poore clerkes for several
monthes with greate attentyon and travaile." This great man, we
have already seen, had an idea of many of the useful arts of life

some years before they were practised.

Here he appears to have had a confused notion of that noble invention, the printing-press. To prevent misconstruction, I should add, that boke in the above passage manuscript, no other books being then known. In other parts of his works, as represented by Chatterton, he speaks of Mss. as contratdistinguished from books; but in all those places it is reasonable to suppose some interpolation by Chatterton, and those who choose it, may read book instead of manuscript; by which this trivial objection to the authenticity of these pieces will be removed, and these otherwise discordant passages rendered perfectly uniform and consistent. This valuable relick shows with how little reason the late Mr. Tull claimed the merit of inventing that useful instrument of husbandry, the drill-plough. I make no apology for anticipating Mr. Barret on this subject; as in fact these short extracts will only make the publick still more desirous to see his long-expected History os Bristol, which I am happy to hear is in great forwardness, and will, I am told, contain a full account of the Yellow Roll, and an exact inventory of Maistre William Cannynge's Cabinet of coins, medals, and drawings, (among the latter of which are enumerated many, highly finished, by Apelles, Raphael, Rowley, Rembrant, and Vandyck) together with several other matters equally curious.—It is hoped that this gentleman will gratify the publick with an accurate engraving from a drawing by Rowley, representing the ancient Castle of Bristol, together with the square tower ycleped the Dongeon, which cannot fail to afford great satisfaction to the purchasers of his book, as it will exhibit a species of architecture hitherto unknown in this country; this tower (as we learn from unquestionable authority, that of the Dean of Exeter himself,) "being remarkably decorated with images, ornaments, tracery work, and crosses within circles, in a style not usually seen in these buildings."—Chatterton, as soon as ever be heard that Mr. Barrett was engaged in writing a history of Bristol, very obligingly searched among the Rowley papers, and a few days afterwards furnished him with a neat copy of this ancient drawing.

[22] This very curious and interesting history may be found in Mr. Bryant's Observations, &c. p. 512. The learned commentator seems to have had the great father of poetry in his eye, who is equally minute in his account of the sceptre of Achilles. See II. A. v. 234. He cannot, however, on this account be justly charged with plagiarism; these co-incidences frequently happening. Thus Thomas Rowley in the 15th century, and Dryden in the 17th, having each occasion to say that a man wept, use the same four identical words—"Tears began to flow."

RESOLUTION AND INDEPENDENCE

AN EXCERPT

By William Wordsworth

I thought of Chatterton, the marvellous Boy,
The sleepless Soul that perished in his pride;
Of Him who walked in glory and in joy
Following his plough, along the mountain-side:
By our own spirits are we deified:
We Poets in our youth begin in gladness;
But thereof come in the end despondency and madness.

THOMAS CHATTERTON

By William Charles Mark Kent

Thomas Chatterton was a poet, born at Bristol on 20 Nov. 1752, was the posthumous son of a poor schoolmaster, who died on 7 Aug. 1752. His parents, Thomas Chatterton of Bristol and Sarah Young of Stapleton, were married on 26 April 1748 at Chipping-Sodbury in Gloucestershire, and had three children, Thomas, Mary (nearly four years his senior), and a brother (Giles Malpas), who died in infancy. Thomas was born in a small tenement immediately behind Pyle Street charity school, of which his father had been master, and was baptised on 1 Jan. 1753 at St. Mary Redcliffe. For nearly two hundred years his paternal ancestors had been hereditary sextons of the church. Chatterton's father has been described by one of his pupils as a roystering and rather 'brutal fellow,' who was remarkable for having so wide a mouth that he could put his clenched fist inside it. He was, however, a man of ability. He was a skilled numismatist and collected several hundred Roman coins, afterwards in the museum of Sir John Smith, bart., of Ashton Court. Southey has preserved 'A Catch for Three Voices' by him (iii. 495) in the 1803 edition of the Works of Chatterton. He read Cornelius Agrippa, affected a belief in magic, and was fond of books.

Chatterton's mother—who was born in 1731 and died on 25 Dec. 1791, aged 60—early in 1753 removed to a house on Redcliffe Hill, opened a dame's school, and took in sewing. Mrs. Chatterton, the poet's grandmother, and Mrs. Edkins, formerly Miss James, who assisted Mrs. Chatterton as a sempstress, and who is usually spoken of as Chatterton's foster-mother, lived with the family. They soon removed to a smaller house, up a court, at the back of No. 50, thenceforth memorable as Chatterton's home at Bristol. Chatterton was at first regarded as stupid. At four he knew but one or two letters of the alphabet. At five he was sent as a day scholar to Pyle Street school, of which Stephen Love became master in 1757. He was soon returned as a dull boy. He was regarded by his mother until the age of six and a half as 'little better than an absolute fool.' One day, seeing his mother tearing up as waste paper an old French musical folio of her husband's, the boy, as she said, 'fell in love' with the illuminated capitals. From that moment his dormant powers seem to have been awakened. He rapidly learned to read, and was taught from the Gothic characters of an old black-letter Bible. At seven he was remarkable for his brightness, and at eight had become an insatiable reader. He sat for hours as if he were in a trance, and would break abruptly into passionate weeping. He even then systematically neglected both food and sleep. At home his favourite haunt soon came to be a dusty lumber-room, overlooking a little back garden. He held this room before long under lock and key as his own exclusively. Another favourite haunt was the church of St. Mary Redcliffe, to which he had at all times ready access. The sexton was the boy's uncle, Richard Phillips, to whom Chatterton had peculiarly endeared himself. His sister has related how, on a pedlar promising to bring presents to herself and her brother, Chatterton answered, 'Paint me an angel with wings and a trumpet to trumpet my name over the world.' Though grave in manner he loved a joke. Edward Smith's aunt Martha spoke of him years afterwards laughingly (Gent. Mag. new ser. x. 603) as 'a sad wag of a boy.' Though at times passionate, he was always singularly winning in his manners. In his eighth year he was nominated to Colston's Hospital, the bluecoat school of Bristol. He was admitted as a scholar on 3 Aug. 1760, on the recommendation of John Gardiner, vicar of Henbury. To his annoyance he was only taught reading, writing, arithmetic, and the church catechism. He told his foster-mother that he could have learned more at home. The junior usher, Thomas Phillips, gave him encouragement. Whenever the boy was released from school he locked himself up in his attic. There he was busily engaged, with a great piece of ochre in a brown pan, a bottle of black lead, and pounce bags of charcoal, in making up heraldic designs and in teaching himself to draw knights in armour, castles, and churches. From his earliest childhood Chatterton had been familiar with the heraldic escutcheons upon the tombs in St. Mary Redcliffe, and intimately acquainted with the peculiarities of various kinds of mediæval palæography. Early in that century seven old oak chests in the muniment room over the great north porch of St. Mary Redcliffe had been broken open by the authorities in order to get at some important deeds. Conspicuous among these chests was a huge one bound with iron, and secured with six keys, 'cysta serrata cum sex clavibus,' known since the wars of the Roses as Canynge's coffer. The keys had been lost, the locks were forced, and the documents were thenceforth left unguarded. Gradually the whole of the contents of the seven receptacles had disappeared, the poet's father carrying off the last sweepings of the muniment room. The boys' bibles were covered by the schoolmaster with many of the parchments, while with the remainder his widow made thread papers for herself and dolls for her children. In the winter of 1762 Chatterton was confirmed by the Bishop of Bristol, and was greatly impressed by the ceremony. It happened at the same time to be his turn for the week to be doorkeeper at Colston's. Then it was that he wrote his first poem, 'On the Last Epiphany, or Christ coming to Judgment.' It appeared in 'Felix Farley's Bristol Journal' on 8 Jan. 1763. Soon afterwards he paraphrased the ninth chapter of Job and several chapters of Isaiah. He became more cheerful after he began to write poetry. As a new year's gift Chatterton's sister gave him at this time a pocket-book, which at the close of 1763 he returned to her filled with writings of his own, chiefly poetical. Two of them, 'A Hymn for Christmas Day' and 'Sly Dick,' both written when he was eleven, have been preserved. He had begun to devote a good part of the few pence given him weekly for pocket-money to borrowing books from the circulating libraries. He hired among others a black-letter copy of Speght's 'Chaucer.' Between his eleventh and twelfth year he drew out a list of over seventy works read by him, chiefly in history and divinity. Meanwhile he had become interested in the Canynges and other Bristol celebrities associated with St. Mary Redcliffe.

His attention was one day awakened by coming upon one of his father's old fragments of parchment then in use by his mother as a silk winder. He exclaimed that he had found a treasure. He then collected all the remaining morsels of parchment anywhere discoverable in the house, and took them to his attic. On 7 Jan. 1764, in 'Felix Farley's Bristol Journal,' appeared his satiric poem, a fable, entitled 'The Churchwarden and the Apparition.' It referred to the vandalism of one Joseph Thomas, then churchwarden of St. Mary Redcliffe. In another part of the same number appeared a letter signed 'Fulford, the gravedigger,' which has been suspected to have been Chatterton's first literary disguise. On 14 April 1764 he wrote another satiric poem on a religious dissembler, called 'Apostate Will.' In the summer of 1764 Chatterton first spoke about certain old manuscripts which he said had come into his possession through his father from Canynge's coffer in the muniment room of St. Mary Redcliffe. He told a schoolfellow, James Thistlethwaite, that he had lent one of these old manuscripts to the junior usher, Phillips, who a few days later showed a discoloured piece of parchment on which was 'Elinoure and Juga,' the earliest produced of the so-called ancient poems, though the latest printed of them all during Chatterton's lifetime. It was first published five years afterwards in the May number for 1769 of Hamilton's 'Town and Country Magazine.' Chatterton had therefore written it when he was no more than in the middle of his twelfth year. Phillips was at once convinced of its antiquity. Chatterton had already adopted an obsolete method of spelling, and adapted to his use a mass of words from the old English dictionary of Nathan Bailey, and from that of John Kersey. With the help mainly of the latter he compiled a glossary for his own purpose in two parts: 1. Old words and modern English; 2. Modern English and old words. From the outset he never had any confidant as to his methods. His success with Phillips encouraged a new experiment. Henry Burgum was then carrying on business as a pewterer, in partnership with George Catcott, at a house now known as 2 Bridge Parade. There Chatterton one day, early in 1767, looked in upon him with the announcement that, among some old parchments from Redcliffe Church, he had just discovered an emblazonment of the De Bergham arms with a pedigree, showing Burgum's relationship with some of the noblest houses in England, and his direct descent from one of the Norman knights who came over with the Conqueror. A few days afterwards Chatterton placed in his hands, neatly written out in an ordinary boy's copybook, 'An Account of the Family of the De Bergham, from the Norman Conquest to this time, collected, from original Records, Tournament Rolls, and the Heralds of March and Garter's Records, by Thomas Chatterton.' Elaborate references were made in it all down the margin to various authorities. Burgum accepted this account of his high lineage as a thing proven, and with it a parchment eight inches square, on which Chatterton had painted an heraldic blazon of the De Bergham coat of arms, and gave five shillings to the discoverer. For a second instalment of the pedigree, brought to him a few days later, continuing it to the reign of James II, he gave another five shillings. On some of the leaves of the first instalment were written two of Chatterton's spurious antiques, 'The Tournament' and 'The Gouler's Requiem.' In the second instalment Chatterton introduced 'The Romaunte of the Cnyghte,' purporting it to have been written in 1320 by John de Bergham, one of the pewterer's ancestors. Burgum went to London, a little while afterwards, to have his pedigree duly authenticated at the Heralds' College, and learned that there was no record of a De Bergham ever having borne arms. The whole affair may be regarded as a schoolboy's practical joke. Chatterton's first conception of the 'Rowley Romance' dated from 1765. Its central figure was an imaginary monk of the fifteenth century, Thomas Rowley, afterwards spoken of as a secular priest at St. John's Church, the friend and confessor of the great merchant and mayor of Bristol, William Canynge the younger. It has been ingeniously suggested (Gent. Mag. new ser. August 1838) that a clue is readily discoverable to Chatterton's selection of the name of Rowley from a passage in Bailey's Dictionary, which accounts for Charles II's nickname of Rowley. An old epitaph in St. John's Church, Bristol, recording the death, on 23 Jan. 1478, of Thomas Rowley, a merchant of that seaport, might as readily have guided him in his choice of the christian name and parish, in 1465, of his purely imaginary Rowley, 'prieste of St. Johan's, Bristowe.' What is most wonderful, however, about the 'Rowley Romance' is that Chatterton produced with his boyish hand the poetical works not of one alone, but of twelve antique poets. While he was preparing the earlier of these elaborate fabrications, he left the school, on 1 July 1767, and on the same day was apprenticed to John Lambert, an attorney of Bristol, whose office at the time was on St. John's Steps. At the signing of his indentures 10*l.* was paid over by Colston's trustees to Lambert. Chatterton's office hours were worse even than his school hours, being from 7 a.m. to 8 p.m. all the year round. He was treated persistently as a mere office drudge, required to sleep with the office boy, and to take his meals in the kitchen. He was allowed every day to spend an hour at his own home, from 8 to 9 p.m. He was only once—upon a Christmas eve—known to have exceeded the prescribed limit, till 10 p.m. Shortly after the commencement of Chatterton's apprenticeship the attorney's office was removed to the first floor of the house now numbered 37 Corn Street, opposite the Exchange. Chatterton had many friends, conspicuous among whom were Thomas Palmer, apprentice to a jeweller in the same house; Thomas Cary, a pipe-maker, called his 'second self;' William Smith, sailor and actor; John Broughton, an attorney, who afterwards collected his miscellanies, and many others. But he confided his secret to no one. He worked regularly at the office. His duties, which were chiefly the copying of precedents, engaged him upon an average no more than two hours every day. But after two years and nine months' occupation he had penned three large volumes: a folio of 334 closely written pages of law forms and precedents, another containing thirty-six notarial acts, and the ordinary book filled with notices and letters; all of them in his symmetrical and clerkly handwriting. The rest of his time was given up to self-education, and to the elaboration of an extraordinary number of his pseudo-antique poems. His studies ranged, according to Thistlethwaite's account (Milles, p. 456), from heraldry to metaphysics, from astronomy to medicine, from music to antiquities and mathematics. On the Sundays he took solitary rambles into the country, whence he seldom returned without bringing back with him sketches he had taken of churches or ruins.

In September 1768 a new bridge had been opened for foot passengers, and it was generally known that in the following November it would be publicly inaugurated. The whole city was startled by the appearance in 'Felix Farley's Bristol Journal,' on 1 Oct. 1768, of an account of the mayor's first passing over the old bridge in 1248. The description purported to have been taken 'from an old manuscript,' and was transmitted to the printer of the journal by one signing himself 'Dunelmus Bristoliensis.' Curiosity was at once awakened as to the source from which this curious document had emanated, the original of which is now at the British Museum. Chatterton shortly afterwards appeared at the newspaper office, and was recognised as the bearer of this singular contribution. He said upon inquiry that he was employed by a gentleman in transcribing certain ancient manuscripts, and that he was at the same time writing complimentary verses to a lady to whom the gentleman in question was engaged. The description, he added, was copied from a parchment procured by his father from the muniment room of St. Mary Redcliffe. Yet Chatterton frankly admitted to a friend of his own age, John Rudhall, that 'he was the author of it' (Milles, 437), showing him afterwards how the appearance of antiquity might be readily counterfeited. He had meanwhile applied, under his now familiar assumed name, to contribute to the 'Town and Country Magazine,' in the next number of which (November 1768) appeared this notice: 'D. B. of Bristol's favour will be gladly received.' Three weeks or a month after the account of the procession over the old bridge had been published, George Catcott, Burgum's partner, heard for the first time, according to his own statement (*Gent. Mag.* 11 Sept. 1788), of certain ancient manuscripts in the muniment room of St. Mary's. Elsewhere he says, less probably, that it was a year earlier (see *ib.* xlviii. 347, 403). Catcott was a bustling, vain, and eccentric man, who boasted that there were no books in his library less than a hundred years old. He now made Chatterton's acquaintance, and received from him, as gifts, one after another of the Rowley poems. First among them in point of time was the 'Bristowe Tragedie, or the Dethe of Syr Charles Bawdin'—four years afterwards published in quarto, as the earliest of all the Rowley poems separately printed. On its being first issued from the press, in 1772, Horace Walpole ascribed it to Dr. Percy, the bishop of Dromore. When taxed with its authorship by his sister and mother, Chatterton from the first acknowledged that he had written it. Soon after this 'The Epitaph on Robert Canvnge' was placed in Catcott's hands, and a few days later the largest of all the so-called Rowley parchments, containing, in sixty-six verses, Rowley's 'Challenge to Lydgate,' the noble 'Songe to Ælla, Lorde of the Castel of Brystowe, ynne daies of yorc,' and Lydgate's 'Answer to Rowley,' It was this dearly prized 'original' that Catcott exultantly took to William Barret [q. v.] Chatterton's first gift to Barrett was 'Turgot's Account of Bristol, translated by Rowley from Saxon into English,' in return for which Barrett lent the boy for a while Thomas Benson's 'Vocabularium Anglo-Saxonicum' and Stephen Skinner's 'Etymologicon Linguæ Anglicanæ' Chatterton knew no Latin, however, though familiar with English poetry and antiquities. On his subsequent introduction, in 1768, to George Catcott's elder brother, the Rev. Alexander Catcott, vicar of the Temple Church, Chatterton obtained access to the Bristol Library. Thence he was enabled to borrow Geoffrey of Monmouth's 'History of the Britons,' Fuller's 'Church History,' and Holinshed's 'Chronicles.' Aided by these later researches, Chatterton gave the final touches to the antique poems that he had been secretly preparing. He gave them to George Catcott and William Barrett. A foreshadowing of one of the earliest of these, written when he was fifteen, was the fragment of a so-called ancient poem entitled 'The Unknown Knight, or the Tournament,' enclosed in his letter of 6 March 1768 to his bedfellow at Colston's, Baker, who had some time before emigrated to Charlestown, South Carolina. He it was for whom, in his explanation at Felix Farley's printing-office, he affected to be copying the antique manuscripts, and for whom he really, before the close of that year, had written ten love poems addressed to Baker's innamorata, Eleanor Hoyland. The information contained in a more highly elaborated poem, entitled 'The Tournament,' was long supposed to have been wholly inaccessible to him save through an old Latin manuscript of William of Worcester; whereas it turned out that these particulars were readily derived by him from a printed record under William Halfpenny's engraving of Redcliffe Church, published in 1746, a copy of which he must often have seen hanging up in the parlour of his friend, Henry Kater, the sugar-baker. Another longer poem, purporting to be written two centuries afterwards by Rowley and John à Iscam, was 'a most merry interlude,' called 'The Parliament of Sprites.' Of another dramatic poem, 'Goddwyn,' two scenes only have been preserved. The subject of 'Goddwyn is continued in the 'Battle of Hastings.' Duplicate copies of 'No. 1' were given by Chatterton to Catcott and Barrett. On being pressed by Barrett to produce the 'original' from which it had apparently been copied out, Chatterton admitted that it was his own composition. But, on being further pressed by Barrett, he poroduced as indubitably Rowley's English version from the Saxon of Turgot, 'No. 2,' a still lengthier instalment. It was for some time a matter of bewilderment how Chatterton could have contrived to make the names of the chiefs correspond so exactly with the 'Roll of Battle Abbey,' the fact being that he had only to turn for them to Holinshed's 'Chronicles.' The 'Battle of Hastings' is surpassed by the tragical interlude of 'Ælla,' which may be accepted as his masterpiece. 'Ælla,' in the poet's handwriting, was in 1768 handed to Catcott in manuscript. Chatterton, on 21 Dec. 1768, wrote to James Dodsley, offering to procure for him several ancient poems, including 'the oldest dramatic piece extant,' written by Rowley, a priest of Bristol, who lived in the reigns of Henry VI and Edward IV, and asking him to direct his answer to 'D. B., care of Mr. Thomas Chatterton.' Having waited in vain for nearly two months, he wrote again to Dodsley, on 15 Feb. 1769, under his own name, saying that on the receipt of a guinea he should be enabled to obtain a copy of the tragedy of 'Ælla' already referred to in his previous communication. It is uncertain whether he ever received any answer from Dodsley. Both these letters were turned up on the clearing out of Dodsley's counting-house, and were first published in 1813 in John Britton's 'History of Redcliffe Church,' pp. 71, 72. On 25 March 1769 he wrote, from Corn Street, Bristol, to Horace Walpole a brief note signed Thomas Chatterton, enclosing, among other curious manuscripts, 'The Ryse of Peyncteynge in Englande,' as having possibly an especial interest for the author of 'Anecdotes of Painting.' The packet, which contained besides some verses about Richard Coeur de Lion, was sent to Walpole under cover to his bookseller, Bathoe. Walpole answered in a long and courteous letter dated 28 March 1769. Walpole spoke of printing

Rowley's poems, and invited further correspondence. Chatterton answered without delay on 30 March, forwarding further particulars as to Rowley and Abbot John, and enclosing additional manuscripts, such as the poem on 'War,' and the 'Historie of Peyncters yn Englande.' He informed Walpole at the same time that he was the son of a poor widow who supported himself with much difficulty, and that he was clerk to an attorney, but had a taste for more elegant studies. The revelation changed Walpole's whole manner; moreover, shortly after the receipt of this second letter, Walpole showed the enclosures to Mason and Gray (*Cole MSS.* vol. xxv. fol. 50 *b*), both of whom at once pronounced them fabrications, and advised their being returned without delay to Chatterton. Walpole, while retaining the manuscripts, wrote to Chatterton, saying that when he had made a fortune he might unbend in his favourite studies. Chatterton, in a brief note dated 8 April, begged for the immediate return of his manuscripts. Receiving no answer to this, he consulted Barrett as to what further reply should be made. He wrote on 14 April, insisting upon the genuineness of the Rowley papers, and requesting their return as documents likely to be of use to his friend the intending historian of Bristol. At the moment of the arrival of this communication Walpole was starting for Paris, and paid no attention to Chatterton's wish. Having been detained in France six weeks, and having then returned to London, more than three months had elapsed when Walpole received from Chatterton a final and haughty letter on 24 July demanding the papers. Walpole calls this note singularly impertinent, while Southey pronounces it 'dignified and spirited.' Walpole now returned all the papers to Chatterton, and 'thought no more of him or them.' Chatterton's feelings are expressed in his lines 'To Horace Walpole,' written in August 1769. Walpole's defence of his conduct, in answer to an attack in Warton's 'History of English Poetry' (vol. ii. § 8), was privately printed at Strawberry Hill in 1779, and afterwards published in the 'Gentleman's Magazine' in 1782.

Chatterton was embittered by the repulse. He satirised all the leading people of Bristol, even those who were the most intimately associated with himself, and to whom he was under some small personal obligations. His derisive poetical 'Epistle to the Rev. Alexander Catcott,' written on 6 Dec. 1769, and his prose 'Postscript to the Epistle,' dated the 20th of the same month, brought their hitherto friendly acquaintance abruptly to a close. One Bristolian alone never had from him other than the most respectful treatment. This was Michael Clayfield, a distiller, of Castle Street, to whom he was first introduced in the autumn of 1769. He it was who lent Chatterton Martin's 'Philosophical Grammar' and one of the volumes of Martin's 'Philosophy.' Thanks to him also, he obtained access to books on astronomy, out of his study of which came his fine metrical celebration of 'The Copernican System.' This appeared in the 'Town and Country Magazine,' to which in 1769 he had supplied in all no less than sixteen contributions. Among these, in the October number, was his affecting 'Elegy on Thomas Phillips,' then recently deceased, formerly junior usher at Colston's Hospital.

Chatterton's position at Lambert's had become at last intolerable. The attorney burnt any manuscripts not on business, calling them 'stuff.' Chatterton at last wrote to Clayfield, avowing an intention of suicide. Lambert intercepted the letter, and at once forwarded it to Barrett, who so earnestly remonstrated with Chatterton, that the boy was moved to tears. It was after this interview that Chatterton wrote to Barrett perhaps the most characteristic letter he ever penned. It is facsimiled (i. cxvii) in the 1842 edition of Chatterton's 'Works,' and may be turned to in the original manuscript in Chatterton's handwriting at the British Museum (5766 B, 75). He says in it that nineteen-twentieths of his composition is pride. The editor of the 1842 edition of his 'Works' (i. cxvi) says that one day he snatched a pistol from his pocket, and, holding it to his forehead, exclaimed, 'Now, if one had but the courage to pull the trigger.' His seven fatalistic lines on suicide were without doubt written about this period. One morning, in the spring of 1770, Lambert found conspicuously placed on Chatterton's desk a document in the boy's handwriting, which is still preserved under a glass case in the library of the Bristol Institution. It is entitled 'The last Will and Testament of me, Thomas Chatterton of Bristol,' and begins thus: 'All this wrote between eleven and two o'clock on Saturday, in the utmost distress of mind, 14 April 1770.' It is a bitter expression of his misery, with sarcastic bequests to his acquaintance.

On Lambert's reading this extraordinary document Chatterton's indentures were at once cancelled. A guinea subscription was got up among a few friends. With barely five pounds in his pocket after paying his fare, Chatterton left Bristol for London by coach on 24 April. His first letter to his mother, dated two days later, gives a graphic description of his journey. Through a cousin, Mrs. Ballance, he obtained shelter in a house in Shoreditch where she was lodging, and the tenant of which was one Walmsley, a plasterer. There he remained for the first seven weeks of his life in town, sharing the bed of the plasterer's nephew, a young man of twenty-four years of age, according to whose evidence the boy hardly ever slept, writing with a sort of fury all through the night. Before his advent to London Chatterton had contributed to several of the leading periodicals. On the first day of his arrival in town he called upon four of these editors or publishers, receiving from them all, as he tells his mother, 'great encouragement.' During the next four months he is known to have written largely in eleven of the principal publications tnen in circulation: the 'Middlesex Journal,' the 'Court and City Journal,' the 'Political Register,' and the 'London Museum;' as well as in the 'Town and Country,' the 'Christian,' the 'Universal,' the 'Gospel,' the 'London,' the 'Lady's,' and the 'Freeholder's' magazines. Such was the rapidity with which he wrote at this time, that of the 444 lines of his satirical poem of 'The Exhibition,' the unpublished manuscript of which yet lies at the Bristol Library, the first line was dated 1 May,

and the last line 3 May, the whole of it having been run off at a heat at Shoreditch. The merest fragment of it (fourteen lines in all) has been printed, the rest having been suppressed as unfit for publication. Chatterton's life, however, was not licentious. He retained his affection for his family. He was abstemious in diet, preferring a few cakes and a glass of water for his meals; drinking tea and disliking hot meat. Chatterton's letters to his mother speak of his literary employments, and show that he was still thinking of his Rowley manuscripts. He wrote squibs, tales, and songs, and tried to rival Junius by letters signed 'Decimus' in the 'Middlesex Journal.' He wrote a letter signed 'Probus,' addressed to the Lord-mayor Beckford [q. v.], which procured him a personal interview with Beckford himself. It appeared in June in the 'Political Register.' A second was written, but was never published; for when Chatterton's hopes were at their highest, Beckford's death on 21 June was announced. At the first shock of those tidings Chatterton, according to Mrs. Ballance, 'was perfectly frantic and out of his mind, and said he was ruined.' Walpole eight years afterwards averred, in his attempted vindication of himself (p. 51), that he had seen in Chatterton's handwriting that second letter to lord-mayor Beckford signed 'Probus,' and a letter of his to Lord North signed 'Moderator,' both of them being dated 20 May, the former a denunciation of, the latter a panegyric on, the administration. The imputation, though based solely on Walpole's assertion, tallies with Chatterton's remark to his sister on 30 May, that 'he is a poor author who cannot write on both sides.' A second letter was sent by Chatterton to his friend Gary, with this endorsement: —
Accepted by Bingley, set for and thrown out of the 'North Briton,' 21 June, on account of the lord mayor's death : —

	£	s.	d.
Lost by his death on this essay .	1	11	6
Gained in elegies	2	2	0
Gained in essays	3	3	0
Am glad he is dead by	3	13	6

Chatterton's change of residence about this time was indicated by the dates attached in the 'London Magazine' to his two 'African Eclogues;' 'Nerva and Mored' being dated 2 May, Shoreditch, and 'The Death of Nicou,' 12 June, Brooke Street. In quitting Shoreditch he bore with him to his new abode near Holborn not only the good opinion of Walmsley and his nephew, but the testimony to his exemplary conduct while under their roof of Mrs. Ballance, his cousin, the plasterer's wife, and her niece, aged 27. Once only during his stay with them, as Crofts states on their testimony (p. 118), did he stay out all night, Mrs. Ballance assuring the author of 'Love and Madness' that on that night to her certain knowledge he lodged at a relation's. There can be no doubt that in removing to Brooke Street he was in search of greater seclusion. There, for the first time in his life, he had a sleeping apartment entirely to himself, in which he could write all through the night. He was by this time beginning to lose heart as to his chances in London. Hamilton, of the 'Town and Country Magazine,' gave him no more than 10*l.* 6*d.* for sixteen songs; while Fell, of the 'Freeholder's Magazine,' gave him the same sum for the two hundred and fifty lines of 'The Consuliad.' The whole of his earnings during May and June could not possibly have exceeded 12*l*. On 4 July he sent to the 'Town and Country Magazine,' with a brief note, signed with his familiar initials, D. B., the last and one of the most exquisitely finished of all his Rowley poems, 'An Excelente Balade of Charitie.' It was rejected. Fortunately he had just then completed the adaptation and expansion of a musical extravaganza called 'Amphitryon,' which he had begun writing nearly a year before at Bristol. In its improved and enlarged form it appeared now as 'The Revenge: a Burletta. Written for Marylebone Gardens it was there acted, not certainly during its author's lifetime, but some time before 1777. It was first published in 1796, twenty-five years after the death of Chatterton. The original manuscript was accidentally discovered in 1824 by Mr. Upcott, one of the librarians of the London Institution, on the counter of a city cheesemonger. In 1841 it was purchased by the British Museum with the manuscripts of Samuel Butler, the bishop of Lichfield. On one of its last leaves is written, in Chatterton's handwriting, a receipt for 5*l*. 5*s*. paid for the copyright by Lutfman Atterbury. Chatterton immediately sent a box of presents to his family, including a china tea-service, a cargo of patterns, a curious French snutilbox, and a tan for his mother, another fan for his sister, some British herb tobacco for his grandmother, and some trifles for Thorne. Two more of Chatterton's home letters have been preserved, both to his sister. On 20 July he tells her besides, 'Almost all the next "Town and Country Magazine" is mine.' On its publication, eleven days afterwards, however, he finds that Hamilton has held almost all his contributions over, and for the few that appear he receives no payment. On 12 Aug. Chatterton addresses to George Catcott the last letter he is known for certain to have addressed to any one. He writes: 'I intend going abroad as a surgeon. Mr. Barrett has it in his power to assist me greatly by his giving me a physical character. I hope he will.' He speaks of a roposal for building a new spire for St. Mary Radcliffe, and concludes: 'Heaven send you the comforts of christianity! I request them not, for I am no christian.' His narrow resources were now rapidly drawing to an end. In his Brooke Street lodgings he had won the affection of all who knew him. Though literally starving he could never be persuaded to accept of invitations, which were fretpnent, to dine or sup. 'One evening, however, according to Warton, 'human frailty so far prevailed over his dignity as to tempt him to partake of a regale of a barrel of oysters, when Mr. Cross observed him to eat most voraciously,' 'Three days afterwards Mrs. Angel. knowing that during those three days he had eaten nothing, begged him, on 24 Aug., to take some dinner with her, 'but' (see Croft, p. 121) 'he was offended at her expressions, which seemed to hint- that he was in want, and assured her he was not hungry,' Withdrawing into his garret at nightfall and quietly locking himself in, death came to him before daybreak on 25 Aug. 1770. When, on his continued non-appearance in the morning, the attic door was broken open, it was fiiund, from the contents of a nearly empty phial still grasped in his hand, that he had died from the effects of arsenic. Barrett, in his 'History of Bristol,' nearly 'twenty years later, says (p. 647) that the drug with which he poisoned himself was opium. But Croft, who nine years before had stated that it was arsenic (*Love and Madness*, p. 122), had heard the facts from the coroner. Covering the floor of the garret were minute fragments of paper which were the torn-up atoms of all the manuscripts that had remained at the last in his possession. Among them in all probability was his manuscript 'Glossary.' It remains still doubtful, however, whether those Chatterton or Rowley poems which are known to have been at one time in existence, but which have never yet been published, such as 'The Justice of the Peace,' 'The Flight; the unfinished tragedy of 'The Dowager,' and that other complete tragedy, a mere fragment of which reached the hands of Barrett, entitled 'The Apostate,' perished on this occasion, or were torn up as 'stuff' by Lambert. Chatterton's remains, enclosed in a shell, were interred in the Shoe Lane workhouse burying-ground on 28 Aug. 1770, as appears from the register of burials at St. Andrew's, Holborn, where the name is entered as 'William Chatterton,' to which another hand has added 'the poet.' Years afterwards, when that site had to be cleared for the building up of the new Farringdon Market, the pausers' bones, all huddled together, were remove to the old graveyard in the Gray's Inn Road. A wildly improbable story about the exhumation and reinterment of his remains at Bristol was first told by George Cumberland in Dix's Appendix A (p. 299), and afterwards reiterated more in detail by Joseph Cottle in Pryce's 'Memorials of the Canynges Family' (p. 293). A still wilder story was put forth in 1853 by Mr. Gutch in 'Notes and Queries' (vii. 138, 139), and which purported to be an authentic record of the coroncr's inquest. on the occasion of Chatterton's suicide. 1*'our years afterwards, however, Mr. Moy Thomas was able to demonstrate, from the parish books of St. Andrew's, Holborn, in the 'Athenæum ' of 5 Dec. 1857, the spurious character of the whole narrative. The books also showed that Chattert on died in the first. house from Holborn on the lefthand side, the last number of all in Brooke Street, No. 39. It is shown by an entry in Chat terton's pocket-book that there were st ill owing to him by the publishers more than eleven guineas for writings of his already in their possession and accepted. Three of his contrfiiutions appeared in the 'Town and Country Magazine' for September, and others in the numbers for October and November, among these latter being his friend Cary's simple but afiecting 'Elegy on Chatterton.' Nearly a year after Chatterton's death, at the first. banquet of the Royal Academy, Horace Walpole heard for the first time from Goldsmith, on 23 April 1771, of the tragic close of the boy's career. Tyrwhitt, the editor of Chaucer, gave to the world in 1777 the first edition of Rowley. Warton, the historian of English poetry, accorded to that monk in 1778 a distinct place among the poets of the fifteenth century; while Dean Milles, the president of the Society of Antiquaries, published in 1782 his superb edition in 4to of the 'Rowley Poems,' with elaborate commentaries in proof of their authenticity. Arguments one way or the other, however, have long since ceased. By internal and external evidence alike Chatterton is now known to have been the one sole author of these productions. The proofs are abundant. The Rowleyan dialect is of no age, but rather, as Mathias expresses it, 'a faetitious ancient diction at once obsolete and heterogeneous.' In the mere penmanship of the so-called originals there is a more than suspicious absence of the old contractions, with a super-abundance of capitals, rare in antique manuscripts. The poems swarm with anachronisms in statements of fact. and in style and metre. There are many plagiarisms, besides, from later writers.

Neale, the author of the 'Romance of History,' truly says (*Lectures*, ii. 75): 'Perhaps there never was a more slender veil of forgery woven than that which he threw around his pretended ancient productions.' Yet forgery is hardly the word; for, after all, the most heinous charge directed against Chatterton can only in fairness be thus summed up now, as it was in 1782, by Henry Maty's 'New Review' (pp. 218-33): 'Gentlemen of the jury, the prisoner at the bar is indicted for the uttering certain poems composed by himself, purporting them to be the poems of Thomas Rowley, a priest of the fifteenth century, against. the so frequently disturbed peace of Parnassus, to the great disturbance and confusion of the Antiquary Society, and likewise notoriously to the prejudice of the literary fame of the said Thomas Chatterton.' Southey's letter in the 'Monthly Magazine' for November 1799, announcing the subscription edition of Chatterton's works, which was eventually published in 1803 for the benefit of his family, secured comfort at last to his surviving relatives, whose only pecuniary benefit from his poems until then had amounted to seventeen guineas. Lewis, a Bristol artist, painted a well-known picture of Chatterton in the lumber-room, which, though a mezzo-tinto, passed eventually into a wide circulation. Two dramas, each entitled 'Chatterton,' have been produced; one in France by Alfred de Vigny, and one in England by Messrs. Jones and Herman in collaboration, which was first performed at the Princess's Theatre on 22 May 1884. A cenotaph was erected, by public subscription, in his native place in 1840, and afterwards re-erected in 1857 (see *Bristol Past and Present*, iii. 348), near the north-east angle of Redcliffe churchyard. Shelley celebrates Chatterton in 'Adonais.' Coleridge dedicates to his memory his most impassioned 'Monody.' Keats inscribes to him lovingly his maiden poem 'Endymion.' Horace Walpole says of Chatterton, 'I do not believe there ever existed so masterly a genius.' Joseph Warton declares that he was 'a prodigy of genius, and would have proved the first. of English poets had he reached a mature age.' Dr. Johnson said of him, 'This is the most extraordinary young man that has encountered my knowledge.' Malone declared him to be 'the greatest genius that England has produced since the days of Shakespeare.' Britton, Southey, Wordsworth, Byron, Moore, Scott, Campbell, have all spoken of him in the highest terms, and Dante Gabriel Rossetti, besides inditing in his honour one of the noblest sonnets in the language (see Hall Caine, *Recollections of Rossetti*, p. 186), speaks of him elsewhere (*ib.* chap. vi.) as 'the absolutely miraculous Chatterton, and declares him to be, without any reservation, 'as great as any English poet whatever.'

Chatterton's appearance has been described by those who were familiar with it. According to them all he was well grown and manly, having a proud air and a stately bearing. Whenever he cared to ingratiate himself, he is said to have been exceedingly repossessing; though as a rule he bore himself as a conscious and acknowledged superior. His eyes, which were grey and very brilliant, were evidently his most remarkable feature. One was brighter than the other (*Gent. Mag.* new ser. x. 133), appearing even larger than the other when flashing under strong excitement. George Catcott describes it as 'a kind of hawk's eye,' adding that 'one could see his soul through it.' Barrett, who had observed him keenly as an anatomist, said 'he never saw such eyes—fire rolling at the bottom of them.' He acknowledged to Sir Herbert Croft (*Love and Madness*, p. 272) that he had often purposely differed in opinion from Chatterton 'to see how wonderfully his eye would strike fire, kindle, and blaze up!'

Eight reputed portraits of Chatterton are said to be in existence. But of these one alone is of indisputable authenticity.

1. 'Hogarth's Portrait of Chatterton,' so entitled, was on view in 1867 at the second special exhibition of national portraits in South Kensington. It was lent by the Salford Royal Museum. To that institution it had been presented a few years previously by Alderman Thomas Agnew, the picture dealer. But it is most certainly not a portrait of Chatterton.

2. Gainsborough is supposed by some to have painted the poet's likeness, solely because of this entry at p. 87 of the artist's biography by Fulcher: 'It is said that Chatterton also sat to Gainsborough, and that the portrait of the marvellous boy, with his long owing hair and childlike face, is a masterpiece.' Two quite inconsistent descriptions of this picture are given in 'Notes and Queries,' 2nd ser. iii. 492, 6th ser. v. 367.

3. Francis Wheatley, R.A., is stated to have painted Chatterton's portrait. But the assertion that he did so rests solely on the fading recollections years afterwards of Mrs. Edkins, as jotted down by George Cumberland in appendix A, p. 317, of Dix's untrustworthy 'Life of Chatterton.'

4. A profile of Chatterton, sculptured in relief by some unknown artist, decorated a rustic monument raised in 1784 in the grounds of the Hermitage, near Lansdowne Crescent, Bath, the residence of Philip Thicknesse.

5. Chatterton is said to have drawn a picture of himself in his bluecoat dress, being led by his mother towards the canopied altar-tomb of William Canynge. No such drawing, however, has been anywhere discovered.

6. An odious fancy sketch, hideously out of drawing and execrably engraved, has for many years passed current among the print-sellers of a portrait of Chatterton.

7. Prefixed to Dix's 'Life of Chatterton,' in the October of 1837, as its frontispiece, was an exquisite engraving, by 11. Woodman, of what purported to be a portrait of the poet drawn by Nathan Branwhite, from a picture in the possession of George Weare Braikenridge. A letter, however, from an obscure Bristol sugar-baker, named George Burge, written on 23 Nov. 1837, to a private friend, first published in the 'Gentleman's Magazine' for December 1838, and twice afterwards in 'Notes and Queries,' 2nd ser. ii. 231, and 2nd ser. iii. 53, declared that this picture was painted by Morris and intended as a portrait of his own son. The portrait was therefore suppressed in a second edition of Dix's book. It is stated, however, in the same place (*Notes and Queries*, iii. 53), that Chatterton's mother wrote a letter (omitted by Dix) saying that she had had her son painted in a red coat by Morris. This is clearly

8. Morris's portrait of Chatterton in a red coat—a cabinet picture representing him in profile to the right, as a child of eleven years of age, with grey eyes and auburn hair flowing on his shoulders. This portrait belonged to Sir Henry Taylor. It was presented by Mrs. Newton, Chatterton's sister, to Southey, in return for his kindness in producing an edition of her brother's works for her benefit (Cottle, *Recollections*, i. 271). Miss Fenwick bought it at South's sale, and gave it to Wordsworth. On Wordsworth's death his widow gave it

to Sir Henry Taylor. It is fairly represented by Goodman's engraving from Branwhite.

Chatterton's works, with one exception, appeared posthumously:

1. 'An Elegy on the much lamented Death of William Beckford, Esq.,' 4to, pp. 14, 1770.

2. 'The Execution of Sir Charles Bawdwin' (edited by Thomas Eagles, F.S.A.), 4to, pp. 26, 1772.

3. 'Poems supposed to have been written at Bristol, by Thomas Rowley and others, in the Fifteenth Century' (edited by Thomas Tyrwhitt), 8vo, pp. 307, 1777.

4. 'Appendix' (to the 3rd edition of the poems, edited by the same), 8vo, pp. 309-333, 1778.

5. 'Miscellanies in Prose and Verse, by Thomas Chatterton, the supposed author of the Poems published under the names of Rowley, Canning, &c.' (edited by John Broughton), 8vo, pp. 245, 1778.

6. 'Poems supposed to have been written at Bristol in the Fifteenth Century by Thomas Rowley, Priest, &c., [edited] by Jeremiah Milles, D.D., Dean of Exeter,' 4to, pp. 545, 1782.

7. 'A Supplement to the Miscellanies of Thomas Chatterton,' 8vo, pp. 88, 1784.

8. 'Poems supposed to have been written at Bristol by Thomas Rowley and others in the Fifteenth Century' (edited by Lancelot Sharpe), 8vo, pp. xxix, 329, 1794.

9. 'The Poetical Works of Thomas Chatterton,' Anderson's 'British Poets,' xi. 297-322, 1795.

10. 'The Revenge: a Burletta; with additional Songs, by Thomas Chatterton,' 8vo, pp. 47, 1795.

11. 'The Works of Thomas Chatterton' (edited by Robert Southey and Joseph Cottle), 3 vols. 8yo, 1803.

12. 'The Poetical Works of Thomas Chatterton' (edited by Charles B. Willcox), 2 vols. 12mo, 1842.

13. 'The Poetical Works of Thomas Chatterton' (edited by the Rev Walter Skeat, M.A.), Aldine edition, 2 vols. 8vo, 1875.

The principal documents in the Rowleyan and Chattertonian controversy are as follows:

1. 'Letter to the editor of the Miscellanies sect. viii. 8vo, pp. 139-64, 1778.

2. 'The History of English Poetry, by Thomas Warton,' vol. ii. sect. viii. 8vo, pp. 139-64, 1778.

3. 'Remarks upon the Eighth Section of the Second Volume of Mr. Warton's History of English Poetry' (by Henry Dampier),8yo, pp.48, 1778.

4. 'Observations on the Poems of Thomas Rowley, in which the authenticity of those Poems is ascertained, by Jacob Bryant,' 8vo, pp. iv, 597, 1781.

5. 'An Examination of the Poems attributed to Thomas Rowley and William Canynge, with a Defence of the Opinion of Mr. Warton,' 8vo, pp. 38, 1782.

6. 'Observations on the Poems attributed to Rowley, tending to prove that they were really written by him and other ancient authors' (by Rayner Hickford of Thaxted), 8vo, pp. 35, 1782.

7. 'Remarks on the Appendix of the edition of Rowley's Poems' (by the Rev. John Fell of Homerton), 8vo, pp. 35, 1782.

8. 'Cursory Observations on the Poems attributed to Thomas Rowley, a Priest of the Fifteenth Century; with some remarks on the commentaries on those Poems by the Rev. Jeremiah Milles, Dean of Exeter, and Jacob Bryant, Esq.; and a salutary proposal addressed to the friends of those gentlemen' (by Edmund Malone), 8vo, pp. 62, 1782.

9. 'Enquiry into the authenticity of the Poems attributed to Thomas Rowley, in which the arguments of the Dean of Exeter and Mr. Bryant are examined, by Thomas Warton,' 8vo, pp. 126, 1782.

10. 'Strictures upon a Pamphlet entitled Cursory Observations, &c.; with a Postscript on Mr. Thomas Warton's enquiry into the same subject' (by Edward Burnaby Greene), 8vo, pp. 84, 1782.

11. 'The Prophecy of Queen Emma; an ancient Ballad lately discovered, written by Johannes Turgotus, Prior of Durham, in the reign of William Rufus; to which is added by the editor an account of the discovery and hints towards a vindication of the authenticity of the Poems of Ossian and Rowley' (by William Julius Mickle), 4to, pp. 40, 1782.

12. 'An Archæological Epistle to the Reverend and Worshipful Jeremiah Milles, D.D., Dean of Exeter, President of the Society of Antiquarians, and Editor of the superb edition of the Poems of Thomas Rowley, Priest, to which is annexed

a Glossary, extracted from that of the learned Dean' (by William Mason, according to a correspondent of the Gent. Mag. vol. lxxxvi. pt. i. pp. 489, 490, but far more probably by John Baynes of Gray's Inn, according to the editorial footnote on p. 489), 4to, pp. 18, 1782.

13. 'Vindication of the Appendix to the Poems called Rowley's, in reply to the answers of the Dean of Exeter, Jacob Bryant, Esq., and a third anonymous writer; with some further observations upon those Poems, and an examination of the evidence which has been produced in support of their authenticity, by Thomas Tyrwhitt,' 8vo, pp. 223, 1782.

14. 'Rowley and Chatterton in the Shades, or Nugæ Antiquæ et Novæ; a new Elysian Interlude in Prose and Verse' (by Thomas James Mathias), 8vo, pp. 44, 1782.

15. 'The genuine copy of a Letter found 5 Nov. 1782, near Strawberry Hill, Twickenham, addressed to the Hon. H—ce W—le,' 8vo, pp. 34, 1783.

16. 'An Essay on the Evidence, external and internal, relating to the Poems attributed to Rowley; containing a general view of the whole controversy, by Thomas James Mathias,' 8vo, pp. 118, 1783.

17. 'Chatterton and "Love and Madness." A Letter from Denmark to Mr. Nichols, editor of the "Gentleman's Magazine," respecting an unprovoked attack made upon the writer during his absence from England, by the Rev. Sir Herbert Croft, Bart.' 8vo, pp. 30, 1800.

18. 'Chatterton's Works, edited by Southey and Cottle' (reviewed by Walter Scott), 'Edinburgh Review,' iv. 214–30, April 1804.

19. 'An Introduction to an Examination of some part of the internal evidence respecting the antiquity and authenticity of certain publications said to have been found in manuscripts at Bristol, written by a learned priest and others in the Fifteenth Century; but generally considered as [*sic*] the supposititious productions of an ingenious youth of the present age, by John Sherwen, M.D.,' 8vo, pp. 137, 1809.

20. 'Chalmers's English Poets' (reviewed by Robert Southey), 'Quarterly Review,' xi. 492–5, July 1814.

21. 'Specimens of the British Poets' (edited by Thomas Campbell), 8vo, vi. 152–62, 1819.

22. 'Chatterton: an Essay, by Samuel Roffey Maitland, D.D., F.R.S.,' 8vo, pp. 110, 1857.

23. 'Essay on the Rowley Poems, by the Rev. Walter Skeat, M.A.,' Aldine edition, ii. vii–xlvi, 1871.

The Chatterton manuscripts in the British Museum are 'Additional MSS. 5766, A, B, and C.' They were left by Barrett, in 1789, to Dr. Robert Glynn, who in 1800 bequeathed them to the trustees of the British Museum. A is a large thin folio containing twelve of the reputed Rowley originals, (1) 'The Storie of William Canynge,' beginning 'Anent a brooklette as I laye reclined,' (2) 'The Yellow Roll,' (3) 'The Purple Roll,' and (6) 'W. Canynges Feast.' B is a medium folio, in which are eighty-six manuscripts, the most remarkable of which are (4) 'The Parliament of Sprites,' (8) 'The Account of the Mayor's passing over the Old Bridge,' (48) and (49) the two letters from Chatterton which Horace Walpole said he never received, but which have clearly stamped on them the evidence of their having passed through the post-office into his possession, (52) 'The Articles of Belief of Thomas Chatterton,' and (75) the letter to Barrett. C is an octavo, consisting of twenty-two leaves of manuscript filled with heraldic and architectural drawings, only a few of which are of any importance. Another notable Chattertonian relic treasured up at the British Museum is the original manuscript of his burletta, 'The Revenge,' numbered among Additional MSS. 12050, all of it in Chatterton's handwriting. At the Bristol Library in the Queen's Road (see its *Catalogue*, p. 311) are, with other Chattertonian manuscripts, the holographs of 'The Battle of Hastings' and 'The Tournament.' At the Bristol Institution, in a glass case, is the poet's 'Last Will and Testament.'

Printed in Great Britain
by Amazon